The
INTANGIBLE SINGING Voice

BY
Glenn White

Copyright © 2013 Glenn White
All rights reserved.

ISBN: 0615757502
ISBN 13: 9780615757506

Library of Congress Control Number: 2013901526
PlayitbyEar
Peekskill, New York

Table of Contents

An Introduction 7
    In the Beginning There Was...Imitation
    Vinyl, Child of the Seventies
    I Love a Piano

Part I: The Singer's Tool Bag 15
    Getting to Know You: Touching the Intangible
    Breath: Breathing Correctly?
    Space: The Width of Your Thumb, A Minimum
    Scales Are Tools
    Are We There Yet? Placement or Vocal Direction
    Say the Words: Articulation
    Musical Mechanics: Approaching a Song Like a Musician

    Mars and Venus in Music (Males and Females)
    Colors of Sound
    Masculinity and the Male Voice
    Musical Theater, Classical Singing, and the Fear of Opera

    The Arch of a Song: Acting in Music

    In Conclusion: Think Less, Feel More—A Paradox

Part II: Learning, Teaching, and Culture.... 65

Studying: How We Learn Patience, Process, Discipline, and Practice
The Three S's
Overthinking It

Pedagogy
How we teach
Cracking: An Occupational Hazard
To Critique or Nurture? That Is the Question
Too Much Talking
A Challenge, You Say?
A New School of Thought

A Culture of Singing 87

Belting, Broadway Musicals, and the Men Who Write Them
Can't Carry a Tune…
In Closing: Serve the Music

Appendix I: Health for the Singer................. 95
Appendix II: Styles of Sound—A Listening List............................ 101

I dedicate this to:

Mrs. Clara DeVries, who encouraged me to sing,

and

Mrs. Beverly Mandell, who encouraged me to write.

An Introduction

In the Beginning There Was...
IMITATION

It all begins with imitation—"mama, dada"—we learn how to speak by imitating those we are surrounded by with the express desire to communicate, with our families, guardians, friends being our first teachers. Perhaps later on we go to a speech therapist to help with a lisp or a stutter, but initially we learn how to speak by imitation solely. No one sits us down and gives us an elocution lesson at the tender age of six months, no, and so it is with singing. We hear a song that we like and sing along. We like the beat; we like the hook. We like the way the singer ascends to the money note. We like the way it makes us feel. It's powerful. Music is powerful. No one teaches us how to do this. It comes with the package. We're the package. Out of the birth canal, given the functions of hearing and speech have not been marred during the development of our very embryo, we can make sound and do. In fact, the very first thing we do out of said canal is just that, make sound. We cry...probably the only time in our existence that crying elicits joy in the others around us, a sign that we are alive, all subsequent cries provoking a myriad of other reactions. Yes, the very first thing we do in this life is make sound, and we don't stop until the fat lady sings.

Vinyl, Child of the Seventies

According to legend, the first song I sang was called "Downtown," by Petula Clark. I even have vague memories of being in my crib singing the hook over and over and over again, "Downtown, downtown," descending a perfect fourth from "down" to "town." I loved music as a child. I loved to sing. I was born in the sixties, but I consider myself a child of the seventies. I did not attend Woodstock; I was six at the time. My parents were not hippies. They were working and raising children and paying a mortgage. My first memory of politics was the president lying to me—Watergate. Another was watching him and his wife play with pandas in Japan. I thought that was cool. I had no cognizance of Vietnam although we were still there. Nor do I have a recollection of the assassination of either Martin Luther King, Jr., or Bobby Kennedy, but what a time in history to be coming into the world. I was born in March of 1964, less than six months after President Kennedy was assassinated, safely tucked away in my mother's womb. No wonder I was three weeks late. Who'd want to come out after that?

As a child of the seventies, I wore leisure suits, ones with snap-button jackets and patterns of giraffes on the shirts—subtle. I carried a transistor radio with me, kind of like the way you see people carrying around iPods today. And I listened to AM radio and prayed they would play my favorite songs while I rode my bike: "Daniel" by Elton John, or "September" by Earth, Wind & Fire. Some of the sounds I heard from my brothers room: Maynard Ferguson, Blood, Sweat & Tears, and Steely

An Introduction

dan. Off my parents' stereo: Stan Kenton, Frank Sinatra, and Broadway soundtracks. Saturdays were spent at Sam Goody, where I purchased LPs and 45s for a dollar each. Later on, I bought sheet music so I could actually learn how to play all the songs I'd been listening to on the piano, from Carole King to the show tunes of Rodgers and Hammerstein.

Vinyl records were a passion of mine. I loved collecting them and keeping up with the latest hits. Listening served as a relief, a comfort, a joy, and a savior. In addition to learning how to play these songs on the piano, I had the privilege of making music in school bands as an instrumentalist. So, it's heartbreaking to hear about the furtherance of music programs being cut from schools. People say, "It's only music..." For many, it's a matter of life and death. I don't know where I would've wound up without it. It helped me survive, and it still does at times. It's a necessity. I'm grateful for the thousands of artists who filled my album rack under my turntable. I still have a lot of them and continue to add more. I have several turntables, one that you can convert analog into digital, plus a CD player, a boom box with a tape cassette deck, a computer, and an iPod—a smorgasbord of the evolution of how we hear music. They all come in handy when I'm in the mood and need a fix: Billie Holiday, Mel Tormé, Kenny Loggins, Michael Jackson, on and on. It takes me out of the ordinary and propels me into another dimension. But any music lover reading this knows exactly what I'm talking about. Listening and playing music teaches me what it is to "be in the moment." I'm in it fully, nothing else matters, and there's no other place I'd rather be.

I Love a Piano

One of my first desires was to play the piano. I had the privilege of receiving one at the age of eight after I had expressed that desire to my folks. Not all are so lucky. I can't tell you how many times after playing publicly the number of adults who expressed sadness in being denied the opportunity to learn or regret because they refused to as children when it was made fully available to them. What can you do? These things can't be forced on children and shouldn't be. I don't believe anyone learns to the full extent when it's nothing but a dreadful experience. It's music, after all; dread should not be part of the equation. And let's face it; youth is also wasted on the young. Hindsight is still 20/20. And concerning the former, it is a shame when kids are not able to play an instrument of their choice. Pianos are expensive, not to mention space moochers, taking up a lot of room in a house. But for the record, there is no substitute for a piano. Though I may be biased, I've heard stories where kids were given a clarinet or cheap violin in its stead...it's not the same. The kid knows it and so does the parent who's trying to make it work. I think the digital age has made some of that easier what with virtual keyboards and so on, in the way that much of technology is making greater opportunities for the exposure and accessibility unto many things. And perhaps this will lessen future generations of saddened and guilty adults lamenting to working pianists.

On the day my piano arrived, I sat down and played "Mary Had a Little Lamb." How did I do that? No one had ever taught me. This is what they call playing by ear. After my rousing rendition of Mary's lamb, I informed my parents that I no longer needed those piano lessons they'd been

An Introduction

talking about; I already knew how to play. This is where I am glad that eight-year-olds were not making executive decisions in my house. I went on to study for the next eight years of my life. However, some people don't. Some continue to learn by solely playing by ear. And some of those people have become famous composers, Jerry Herman and Irving Berlin to name two. Clearly, there is great merit in this path as well. Where would pop culture be without the melodies of "Hello, Dolly!" and "God Bless America"?

When you play the piano, you become very popular, especially with girls who dream of becoming singers. And so, a good bulk of my time in high school was spent in one of the three practice rooms in the music department arranging and transposing songs for talent shows, auditions, and recording demos with and for said girls. In private I wrote and sang my own compositions, until one of those girls having heard me suggested that I might be interested in studying with her voice teacher. So, in the spring of my junior year, I began to; I was seventeen. And by the fall of my senior year, I had improved so that I now had a newfound confidence to audition for the school show and later on competed in the New York State School Music Association, better known as NYSSMA. For even with all the singing along to records that I had been doing most of my life, I often felt unable when it came to reaching higher notes, especially while singing along to pop music. This is where imitation can become limiting, and one must be shown other ways, methods, or tools—what is known as skill or technique. The training that I had received had now propelled me into a new arena. Whereas before I had only seen singing as something I had a natural inclination for, I was now considering pursuing it on a professional level.

Part I:
The Singer's Tool Bag

Part I.
The Singer's Toolbox

Getting to Know You: Touching the Intangible

When a person begins to train his or her singing voice, what he or she is embarking upon—initially unbeknownst to him or her—is a getting in touch with inner sensations; it is the crux of the work that a singer does. This is because the instrument is inside of the singer. It is internal, unlike any other musical instrument, and because of this, it is intangible. You cannot hold it like a saxophone. You cannot touch it like a piano. You cannot pluck it like a violin. And you cannot press your lips into it like a trumpet. Therefore, the closer you become with your internal sensations, your very anatomy, the greater the control and mastery you can begin to attain. When young singers first enter training, they come in all ears. After all, their ears are all they've had thus far as a way to gauge if they are making the "right" sounds. But when young singers enter training, they are now in a room with another pair of ears. As that other pair of ears, I begin to direct the singer to trust these inner sensations as a newer primary way to gauge. With their ears now working in tandem, they begin to build a sense of security that will stand the test of time. It's an inner anchor. Also, how we hear ourselves is not how others hear us; therefore, our very own hearing is deceptive and not to be fully trusted. Listening to recordings of ourselves is always good and useful feedback.

Other musicians deal with both their instrument(s) of choice and their anatomy. Woodwind, brass, and reed musicians deal with something called an embouchure. This is how they position their mouths around the mouthpiece while blowing the proper amount of air through their instruments, controlling pitch, volume, and quality. This alone can take years. I played alto sax for many years; the inside of my bottom lip took a beating for sure. But the point is, these kinds of musicians must learn to coordinate mouth, tongue, lips, and pulmonary system, while pressing the right keys or valves. Some, like clarinetists, also have to make sure they are properly covering the holes, or all will go awry. All this while trying to keep the back, shoulders, arms, and legs relaxed. Easy? No way. String players are a mystery to me, simply because I have no experience with these instruments. What I've learned is that the amount of tension you press on the strings with your fingertips is key, while bowing with the other hand. Imagine how difficult it must be to learn how to keep shoulders, neck, and back relaxed while doing this and remembering to breathe. The skill involved in playing a musical instrument is tremendous and a constant balancing act. And, like anything, people build memory in their muscles, which in time takes over like autopilot, becoming second nature and making it look effortless to us, the audience. But anything that is made to look effortless took much effort to get there. And so it is with a good singer. How uncomfortable is it to watch a singer while fearing if he or she will make it to the high note? Very, right? You don't want to be that kind of singer. If you, the singer, feel secure, so will the listeners; all the more reason to get to know yourself, from the inside out, learning to touch the intangible.

Part I

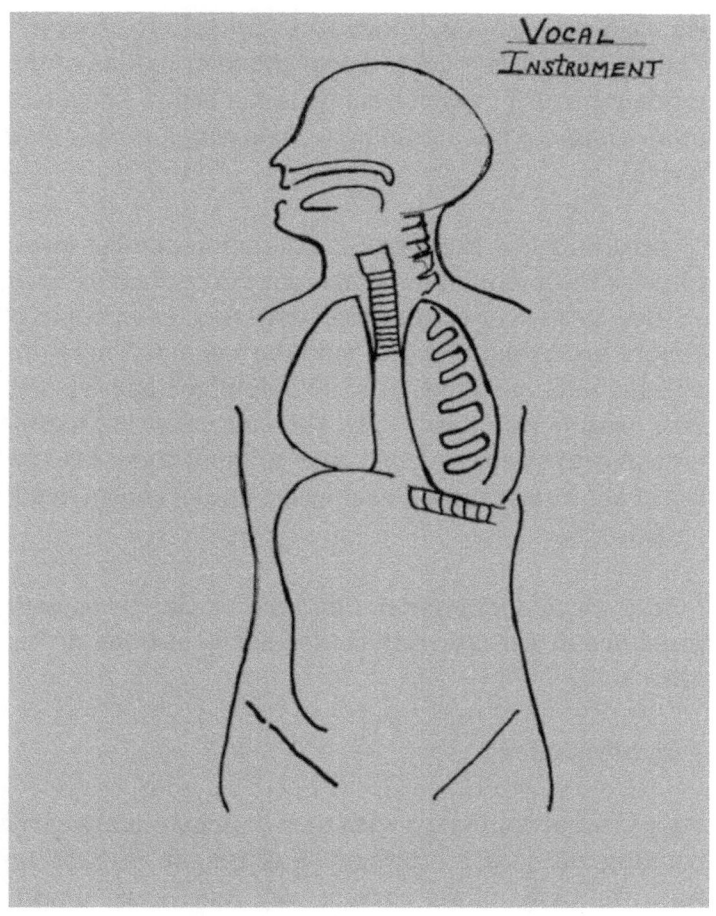

Breath: Breathing Correctly?

I have often found it off-putting to be suddenly taught "how to breathe" upon entering anything from a yoga class to a voice lesson. Hadn't I been doing fine on my own all this time? I mean, I'm still standing, so I must've been doing something right...right? And then suddenly there is a stranger putting his* hands on my stomach or rib cage while saying things like, "See?...Here...Feel it?" Thusly, when I've tried to adopt the instructions of the teacher, it's as if I've been set up to fail before I begin. In other words, if I'm not doing it their way, I'm not doing it right.

Breathing is a vital organic act, and unlike the involuntary functions of other vital organs in our bodies, such as the digestive or cardiovascular system for example, it is both an involuntary and voluntary action. There are actually mammals that exist, like dolphins and whales, who breathe voluntarily only. Therefore, they are hardly ever able to sleep. We don't have to think about breathing in order to breathe, like they do, until it comes to the singing voice.

(*After much deliberation, I decided to take turns with pronouns in fairness, rather than solely use one or the other.)

A Breath Divided

My personal confusion with breath began in my early training days as an actor. I was taught to breathe from the belly as the correct way, known as "diaphramatical breathing." In putting the onus on the belly, I abandoned my rib cage entirely to the admonition and warnings of my teachers as the "shallow or high clavicular breath." I was trained that my chest should never move. And so, I trained diligently in this way for a number of years as a muffled voice inside of me gasping for air kept asking, "What respiratory organ lies in my stomach?"

Part I

Later on, as a singer in training, the focus was on the rib cage, particularly, lower down. I was taught to expand the ribs on the inhale and try to keep them out upon making sound or the exhale. And so I tried—and poorly, I might add—to imitate what my teachers seemed to do so effortlessly with their own bodies; but what about the belly? Was I now to completely abandon the belly for the rib cage? Or now was I only to breathe from the belly when speaking and from the rib cage when singing? Truly, a breath divided.

Breath Memoir

When I was a child, I had an anxiety that I might suddenly stop breathing. It would send me into a panic, and I would then take a number of very deep, conscious breaths in an effort to calm myself down. In time I learned that reminding myself that my body had been breathing fine on its own (involuntarily) quelled the anxiety and allowed my body to normalize. In retrospect, I attributed this fear to chronic childhood bronchitis. When I was a child, my nose would be so clogged that I would only be able to breathe through my mouth. When a person can only breathe through the mouth, he gets dried out and never feels like he can ever get a full breath. It is a terrible feeling. However, it built in me a compassion for teaching breath, especially to people who have suffered from asthma or other respiratory illness. I learned particularly with asthmatics that although they may no longer suffer from it, as many outgrow it, they still deal with the patterns it leaves behind that can limit them when it comes to using their voices. And therefore I say, paying attention to any student's breathing apparatus is a significant piece of work because we are all different.

I think we have all been holding our breath unconsciously for years as a reaction to the many stresses life throws our way. And I believe that it starts as early as elementary school when the teacher calls upon us to give the "correct" answer. Reading that alone might make you hold your breath. Sometimes in a voice lesson, students will suddenly become light-headed, not being used to all the sudden oxygen they are taking in. But this is a good thing; the wooziness will pass as their lungs are being introduced to more oxygen. Sound is made on the exhale. The more one releases air out of the lungs, the greater can one fill the lungs up. This is not only beneficial for singing but clearly for one's health as well.

Anatomy 101

If someone had shown me back then what I know now, it might've saved me from a lot of confusion. What's really happening when we take a breath? Where is it actually going? When breath is drawn through the nose or mouth, it descends into the trachea (windpipe), which then divides into two separate bronchial tubes. It does not descend down the esophagus and into the stomach, as some of us were led to believe. Therefore, there is no lung in your gut! There is further distribution of oxygen divided into smaller vessels, called lobar bronchi. These insert into the separate lobes of each lung. There is further distribution of air into even smaller segments called, alveoli. Then with the help of capillaries surrounding the alveoli, oxygen and carbon dioxide diffuse. There is an exchange of gas. Carbon dioxide is removed by way of the exhale, while capillaries help move the freshly oxygenated blood into your

Part I

circulatory system. All of this takes place because of the involuntary action of the diaphragm. When breath is taken in, the diaphragm (which resides in your thorax, or rib cage), having already taken descent, makes room for that new air that was caused by this vacuum affect. Then, counterintuitively, it rises to help expel air out of the lungs. This is the involuntary action that goes on when we're awake and when we're asleep. This along with all the other involuntary functions of our awesome anatomy is what keeps us thriving; and to think, we don't have to give it one thought. In fact, thinking about it wouldn't add or take away from it, not one jot or tittle. However, it is surely something to come to appreciate.

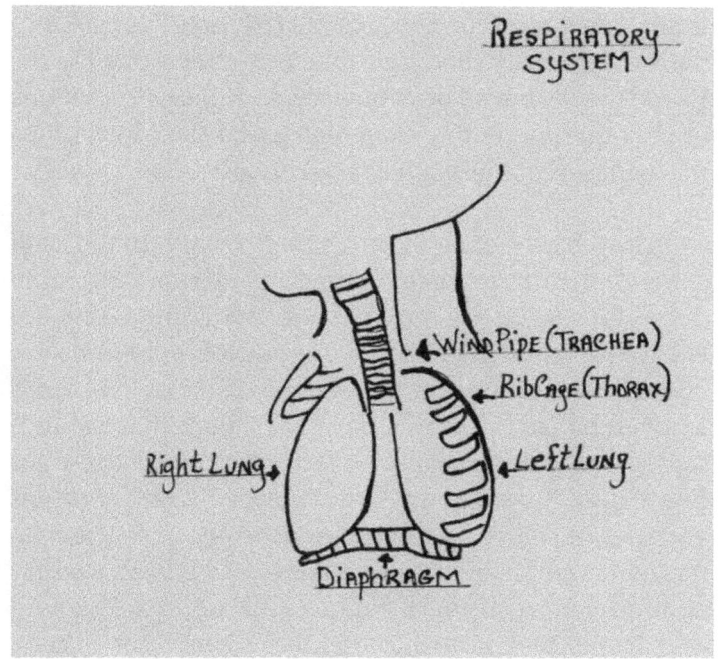

A Balanced Breath

I came to learn that the avoidance of the high clavicular breath (or the shallow breath that I spoke about earlier) was propounded by teachers for the sake of the exhale and not the inhale. If one is to breathe shallowly, as with the high clavicular breath, termed from the bones that lie on top of the rib cage (clavicles), one can get all the air he or she needs. However, when one is singing, there is not a sufficient amount of musculature in that region to support or help control the flow of air. Therefore, it is logical to say that from where one breathes, one will also support—hence the focus in my training on both the belly and the lower ribs. Through many years of trial and error, I have come to this conclusion: a breath that is drawn from both the chest cavity (rib cage) and accompanied by a belly that is pliable as it goes along for the ride is the best of all possible worlds. Hence, it is not one or the other, but both—expandable ribs and a loose, flexible belly—that make a balanced breath.

In my experience as a teacher, I have found that achieving this balanced breath is easier said than done. We live in a compartmentalized culture where we are just figuring out that our bodies and minds are connected. About time. So, with all walks of life comes a mixed bag of breathing patterns. For some, expanding the belly is no problem, whereas others are tight as a drum. A young man who works diligently on his abs will be reluctant to let that area go; so will a classically trained dancer who has been taught to use her abdominals to support balance and agility. This will only leave the rib cage to do all the work. For others, they are locked in their ribs and only have the belly for release and support on their sound, and so on and so on. This is where gravity comes in very handy. The most natural way to find ease and relaxation on the breath is to simply lie on the floor with knees up, feet flat, and just breathe. You can even do it when getting ready for sleep. Take a few conscious breaths, and observe the natural rise and fall of the torso (ribs and belly). Enjoy the relaxation and fullness of breath you can achieve as you allow gravity to do the work for you.

Support

With time and sufficient practice, people are able to bring this newly found breath to a standing position. For those who can find their breath already on their feet, I tell them to go into the "quintessential singer's pose." I spent many voice lessons as a student in this position: hands wrapped around mid to lower ribs with fingers draped across the belly. When one has her hands in this position, it sends a signal to the brain that brings security, confidence, and calm, a mental anchor. This helps the singer relax, especially if she is encountering a rougher section of music to get through. But whether the phrases are hard or not, it gives the singer the sense that she is going to make it. Sensorially speaking, this is the most advantageous place when it comes to understanding how the body works on the voice. When you put your hands in this position, you can feel how the body breathes, and you can feel how the muscles of the respiratory system engage upon making sound. For it is from this place that breath is drawn, and it is also from this place that you will support your sound. Try it: breathe into your hands and sing.

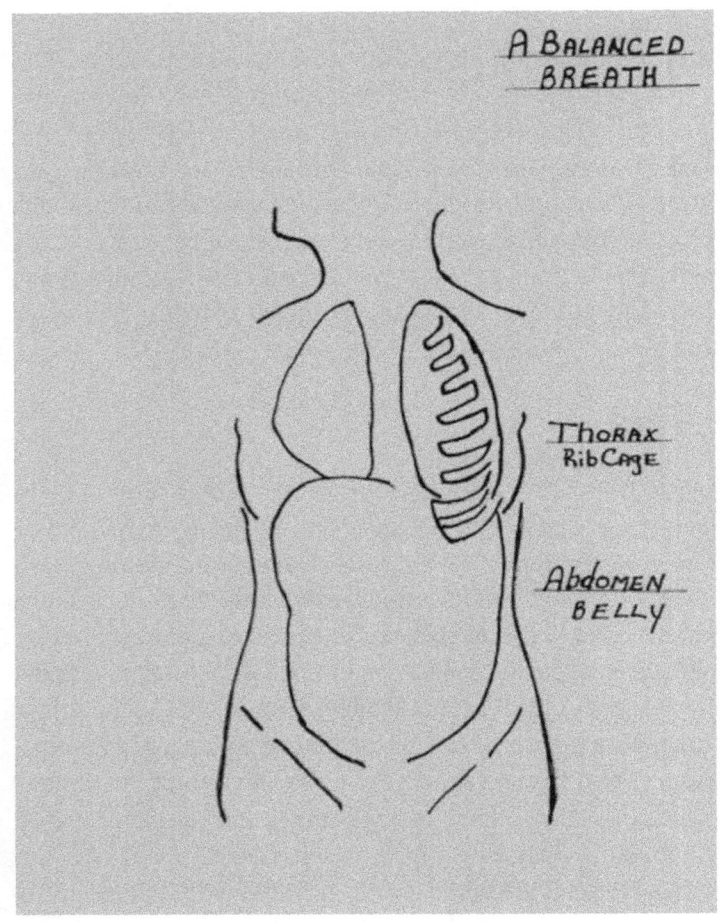

Singer's Breath

The general misconception about the singer's breath or inhale is that before a phrase of music, one must take a huge one in order to get through it. Practically speaking, there will hardly ever be enough time for that. Technically speaking, a big breath will work against the singer. As students are practicing scales and music, they are learning how to distribute air over sound, what is known as breath control. With the singer's breath, economy is key. In other words, it's important to know that a little goes a long way. Nor do you need bigger breaths in order to nail higher notes. Take in what you need, and then figure out how to place them.

I liken the singer's inhale to the breath one takes before leaving a message on a cell phone. We all know *that* breath. Try it before a phrase of music or scale. Also, if you're having trouble making it to the end of a phrase, there is no law against taking two staggered breaths. Remember, pushing through by squeaking a phrase out on one breath teaches you nothing and only cultivates tension, and with breath, relaxation is key.

Males, Females, and Gravity

Men and women have different centers of gravity. Women's are lower, while men's are higher. So, when women are breathing on voice, they will feel it working lower down in the pelvic region, where men will feel it higher up in the solar plexus, just below the sternum. And that is not to say that men will not feel breath down in their pelvic region or women in their solar plexus. These are just primary places of breath, as gravity works with each gender specifically, while the quintessential singers pose still works for both.

What's the Diff?

What's the difference between the usage of breath when we speak and when we sing? For me, there is only a greater usage of my breath when I sing because it is sustained sound. I say to students that the closest they will ever come to singing in their speech would be Shakespeare. It requires, first and foremost, a greater usage of your voice. Also, it's poetry, so it's metered like music. And, like singing, it requires one to speak long lines on one breath, like singing through a melodic line. Yelling is close to singing because it is also more sustained than regular speech, but do me a favor: learn how to do it right so you don't hurt yourself.

Is breathing different in the arts than in our normal, everyday usage? In the golden era of theater, there were foot mics solely on a stage, so as far as projection went, people really had to learn how to engage their bodies in a very unnatural way, so they could be heard at the back of the house. So, yes, at one time I believe that was true. Today that is not so, with body mics hanging visibly outside of a performer's mouth, allowing one to speak in a more conversational tone. Should you get a gig somewhere where they do not have body mics, you'll learn to how to "play to the balcony" by utilizing more of your air. It's good to know how to do both.

Space: The Width of Your Thumb, A Minimum

When I was studying as an actor, they made us put the width of a cork between our top and bottom teeth while we managed to make sound in voice and speech. This technique forced us to keep space in our mouths while working our lazy tongues.

As a singing teacher, I found the equivalent to this is simply the width of your own thumb. Mind you, this is the minimum of space needed even when singing down low in your talking register, i.e., chest, neck, mouth resonance.

As you ascend on a scale, the space will become longer as the jaw descends, depending, of course, on the vowel. And thereby the thumb will no longer be needed. Also, once the mouth becomes conditioned to this minimal thumb space, you won't even need to put your thumb between your teeth. You will have trained those muscles to do it on their own.

The most important direction of space to build in your singing voice is a vertical one. As the voice ascends, the jaw descends. With this kind of setup, the voice is enabled to go in any direction a style may take it. (Imagine pulling a rubber band in either direction, the top representing the voice, the bottom representing the jaw.) Without this habitual space, the singer will always be left to compensate by pushing and whatnot in order to achieve the rigorous demands of music. Space sets it up so that the air can support the sound. This juggling of space and air comes easier with time and practice.

One can also try to achieve this minimal amount of space by simply saying "Ah," like when you're at the doctor's office. If one doesn't begin with this space, the chance of producing sound higher up, comfortably, is nil.

A few easy warm-ups:

My mouthpiece, the jaw

Placing a hand on each side of the face, drop the jaw to that "ah" position talked about in the previous section, and let air out through the mouth as you take a new breath through your nose. This feels good, as it begins to allow the jaw to unwind—the palm of each hand cradling the cheeks—with mouth open while breathing. It's not a bad idea to figure out on a scale from one to ten where your jaw tension lies, where one is the least and ten is the most severe. Then, place hands on the sides of the face and let the jaw hang. Just breathe.

Hiss: A slow, steady stream of air

Remember when you were a kid, and you'd slowly let air out of a balloon? Placing your teeth gently together, take a breath and let the air out in the same way, controlling the rate of speed; you want a slow, steady stream. By doing this, you'll make a hissing sound. You'll also let out more air than normal and thusly be able to fill your lungs even more, giving yourself a full breath. Try this at least three times in a row. Breathe in, hiss out, breathe in, etc. As you do this, place your hands in the quintessential singer's pose, and feel the expansion and release. This is a nice way to get connected to your breath before you even utter a sound and is a great way to practice breath control. It also feels good and is enormously relaxing.

The Nose Knows

There is great benefit to breathing through your nose. It literally warms up the voice by humidifying the air. Eventually, you must get used to breathing from your mouth when you sing. It's just practical and makes singing easier; however, starting from the nose is relaxing, beneficial, and a great way to connect to your air from the get-go, whereas you may not feel that same connection from the mouth.

(These exercises can be done standing, sitting, or lying down. I think all singers should learn how to sing in all three of these positions, though some will beg to differ. Pick the position that is most beneficial to you and get to work.)

Vertical Versus Lateral

I say to my kids, "Go long...then go wide." What is this, football? Look, with singing, you gotta go long before you can go wide. If you try to sing everything, particularly the *i** (as in *bee*) vowel, by going sideways with your mouth, aka, a smile, you're going to run out of room and also kill yourself. If you go long with your mouth, or vertical, then you can always spread your mouth higher up, having plenty of room or space. To experience this spatial setup, put the palms of your hands against the cheeks of your face while you're doing scales, or even when singing a song. This will begin to train your mouth to go long before it goes wide. Lateral space only will become limited quickly, so remember to go long and then go wide. HUT!

(*As shown in the International Phonetic Alphabet or IPA)

How High Can You Go?

This national obsession with high notes makes me want to close down shop and live in a tent, carving wood and growing herbs on a mountaintop.

I will get into this cultural phenomenon later on, but in the meantime, I understand the need to improve said high notes. They're hard, mostly because they resonate in a more ethereal place of our bodies, somewhere between the nasal resonator and the crown of the head. Here's the thing, if you begin with that minimal space just talked about and allow the jaw to descend as you move up in your range, you will find your high notes and be able to improve them.

And lastly, some are sopranos and tenors; some are mezzos, baritones, and altos. Once you figure out what you are, accept it and sing your potential high notes well.

Scales Are Tools

We latch onto the sounds we like. At a very early age this happens. We hear a song sung by a certain singer, and we imitate it as a natural response to our admiration for it. And so we begin latching onto the sounds we like. Since the singing voice is innate, our earliest voice lessons begin by this form of imitation, well before we ever slap down the cash for a real voice lesson. That's why, in my experience, a guy who goes up in his range easily or a gal who belts naturally has easily fooled me. Often, it doesn't necessarily mean that they know what they're doing. No, they're just doing what they do, which they learned from imitating a singer who they heard growing up, latching onto the sounds they liked. However, if one wants to go further with his or her singing than the shower or car stereo, one must learn the instrument the way any woodwind, brass, percussion, or string player would. But instead of learning what string to press or what valve to push, a singer learns how to press his or her buttons by exploring his or her resonators. And one of the ways one does this is by doing scales. And this is where the crowd boos and hisses at me. I know, I know. But don't hate me because I'm a beautiful teacher!

Part I

Most people new to voice lessons or any kind of music lessons do not understand why they have scales thrust upon them by a teacher. So here's why for voice lessons. Doing scales:

- Warms up the voice
- Increases one's range
- Helps one navigate through registration changes
- Teaches one about placement and breathing
- Increases stamina (singing is a lot more physical than many people think)
- Should help one be able to sing all the vowels from the bottom to the top of one's range, thereby lining up all the vocal ducks in a row

How does a singer get better at scales? How does a ballerina get better at barre work? How does one get to Carnegie Hall? Practice, practice, practice!

Are We There Yet? Placement or Vocal Direction

Remember sitting in the back of your father's car while he refused to pull over to get directions at the behest of your worn-out mother? Ah, those were the days...Like it would've killed 'em to ask for help. Why the trip down memory lane? Well, what happens when you don't get the right directions? You get lost. And what happens when you get lost? You get incredibly stressed, scared, and waste gas! And at these prices...

Smell an analogy coming on? Well, it really is no different with a singer. As you navigate through a piece, you may get lost along the way. So, vocal direction, mostly known as placement, will be highly necessary. But where does one find this direction? Certainly not at a gas station. Since the singing voice is inside of each person, and there are no keys to press or strings to pluck, singers must go inside themselves feeling for vibrations through resonators.

All through the day when we speak we are vibrating. If you place a hand on your chest, neck, or top of head, you're bound to feel vibration in one, two, or all three places. (Go ahead and try this while speaking.) So it goes when we sing. The singing voice vibrates between the chest cavity and the crown of the head, depending on vocal range (bass, soprano, etc.), more in some areas, less in others. Beginning from the chest, place your hand on the following: neck, mouth, nasal (nose), forehead, and crown. And moving downward: crown, forehead, nasal, mouth, neck, and chest. Then try placing a hand on each as you sing: chest, neck, mouth, nasal, forehead, and crown, and then crown, forehead, nasal, mouth, neck, and chest. At the beginning, some areas may feel easier to detect than others, but in time, you'll become better acquainted with those areas as well. As you begin to move through scales and pieces of music with increasing awareness of these places of resonance or vibration, you will be better able to place sound particularly in more difficult sections with the aid and help of your teacher, of course. Soon you will be navigating with this new map and know exactly where you are headed measure to measure. Get to know these places, and soon more security and confidence will build. Consider it your vocal GPS.

Part I

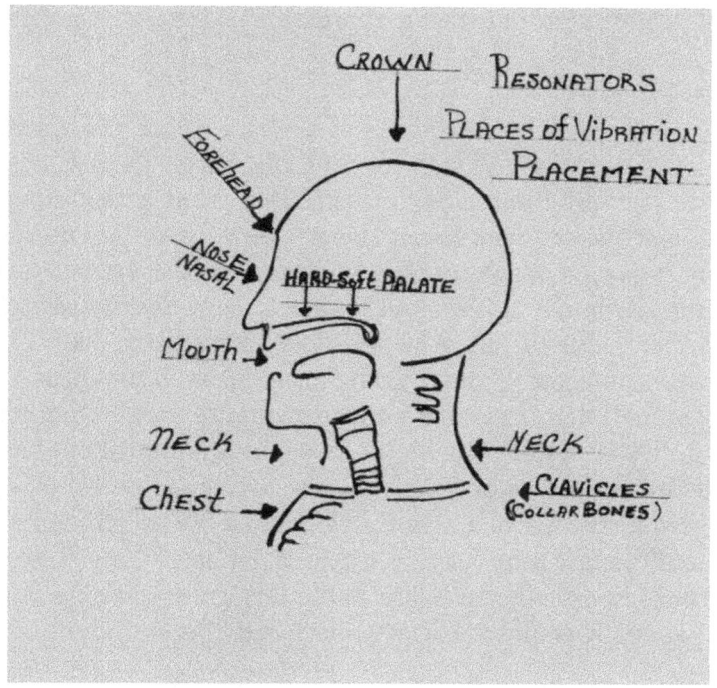

Say the Words: Articulation

There was a pop song, years ago, that I loved. And in it there was a lyric that I swore went like this, "As he rises to her apartment house." Then, as it goes, I embarrassed myself by singing these lyrics out loud in front of a friend one Friday night as we drove around aimlessly. After she stopped her annoying giggling, she told me that the lyrics went, "As he rises through her apology." I stood corrected but still continued to sing my own incorrect lyrics. I liked them better. Why have we all found ourselves in these positions? Could it be an overabundance of wax in our ears? Static? Instruments drowning out the singer? Mediocre articulation? All of the above?

The Intangible Singing Voice

There's an old Italian expression that goes, "Sing as you speak."

In the rock and pop world, lyrics aren't the most important thing. A favorite song can roll by for decades till one day I might ask myself, "Hey, what is that song about? What is she saying there?" We don't care as much because it's not about that, it's about the beat, it's about the rhythm, and it's about the hook. However, there are other fields of pop where it does matter, like country, blues, folk, etc. If you're going for a career in the theater, you had better make damn sure you are articulating in the clearest way possible, because there it is all about the words and the story line. And also for a good percentage of your theatrical audience it will most likely be the first and the last time they ever hear it, let alone how clever and fast-paced scores are being written these days, so you really want to be as clear as a bell.

Since the singing voice is merely an extension of the speaking voice, studying voice and speech is beneficial. Any student I've had who has done so has a good foundation for learning how to sing. They have an understanding of breath, placement (resonators), and articulation. They have learned how to work their tongue, lips, and teeth over consonants and vowels. And so it is for the singer. You might look at singing as a heightened version of speech. And if pop singers want to sing with bags of marbles in their mouths because it's more about what they feel than what they say, so be it. But, if you want not only to be heard but understood as well, learn how to move your lips and tongue over consonants and vowels and say the words!

Part I

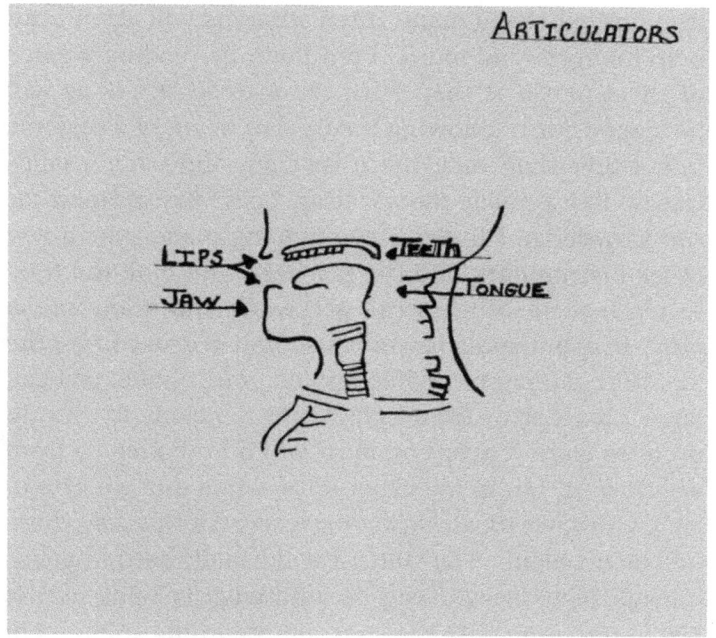

Musical Mechanics: Approaching a Song Like a Musician

A Note on Music Theory

Had my parents not insisted on piano lessons upon the arrival of that piano (see: I Love a Piano), I would've been one of many who played an instrument by ear, which I already had a natural inclination for. There's something magical about playing by ear, the ability to plunk a melody out of thin air. There are many musicians, famous and anonymous, who only play by ear. And, as I've mentioned earlier in the Introduction, there is great merit to it. It has behooved many. Often students will ask if I can help them to read music. I tell them by reading a piece of sheet music as they learn the melody of a song will be a good start, following the up and down of a melodic line. Other than that, there isn't any time. It's a voice lesson, not a music theory class. I am very grateful for the knowledge I learned by studying piano plus a few other instruments, and the teachers who took the time to teach them. Singers can get away with a lot, unlike other instrumentalists who must read in order to get the job. With a good recording app on your phone, you can have a teacher or friend plunk out a melody for you in order to learn it properly. Most will lift the melody from a recording, but in my experience, when one goes on to sing with a live musician having learned it this way, there will be problems. The student will usually second-guess himself, as he tries to reckon with what is being played live in the room with the constant recording spinning in his head. Therefore, there is a crack in his security and confidence. The ground is unsteady. Learning the melody from the actual written music provides an anchor. You know where you stand with the melody without a doubt. The only exception where I have found it more helpful to learn from a recording is with pop music. Often what the singer does on a recording is never fully transcribed on the page, as it can be a bit square. A fine balance of both is best, while still learning structure, tempo, rhythms, and certain melodic lines from the written music.

A number of years ago, I found myself standing in front of junior high school aged students, teaching music theory and sight reading in a performing arts program in New York City. As I imparted beginner theory unto them, I could see eyes rolling accompanied with increased sighs and fidgeting. I remembered how music theory could feel daunting for me and my classmates, just incredibly difficult to wrap our brains around, and now here I was, teaching it. I had become the dreaded theory teacher. What had I done wrong to deserve this? (I asked the gods!) And as much as I tried to "Patch Adams" it out, in order to make it more palatable to them, nothing seemed to work. I began to feel like Sidney Poitier in the first forty-five minutes of *To Sir, with Love* on a loop. No one would be making a Lifetime movie of this teacher's life. Subsequently I left that teaching position and never looked back.

Honestly, I think the best way to learn music theory is while learning how to play a musical instrument. At least then there will be some payoff as one is making music, rather than approaching it like some math problem in calculus, no offense to math-heads. The best suggestion I can offer up to those who have no musical training is to take some beginner piano lessons. Also, joining a choir, chorus, or an a capella group can teach one much from the sheer repetition of reading and working on music from rehearsal to rehearsal. In the meantime, based on my experience as a teacher, coach, and accompanist, here's some food for thought a singer should work on when approaching a piece of music as a musician.

Entrances, Cutoffs, Rhythm, and Breath Marks

So after you've learned the melody properly, there are things you'll want to become better acquainted with, like entrances and cutoffs. In other words, do you come in on the downbeat, and how long do you hold this note out for? These are entrances and cutoffs. Rhythm is a whole other language. You can begin to learn the value of a whole or quarter note, but if you don't for now, you can learn to count as you sing or "feel it." Most people wind up "feeling it." Whatever the modus operandi, it is significant that you're coming in on time and not holding out notes longer than they're written. Those are common mistakes. In singing, economy is essential. You don't want to hold out a phrase any longer than it needs to be. Save yourself, as you've got a whole piece to get through. Once you've gotten the melody, entrances, and cutoffs under your belt, you can begin to decipher where you're going to breathe. And despite the written rhythm, you'll wind up shaving a note by an eighth here, a quarter there, especially in pieces where composers do not consider that singers have to breathe because, you know, they're human. You'll begin to negotiate the timing of a breath by making sure you get enough air to make it through the next phrase. It's completely acceptable to cheat in this aspect, as it'll make for a better vocal and the absence of an EMT crew to resuscitate the singer at the end of the concert...not good for business.

The standard symbols for a breath mark are a check mark or apostrophe. I've always used a check mark. Whatever you use, do it, because here's the thing: breathing is of the accumulative effect. If you don't take the time to make conscious choices on where to breathe, you will breathe haphazardly. Then don't wonder why you have trouble finishing a phrase later on in a piece, or nailing a high note. Eventually the wrong way becomes muscle memory, and until you fix that, you will be subjected to barreling through, dreading every hairy turn. Students will say, "It's obvious where to breathe." I say, "Some are, but some aren't." I also say, "Put 'em in, the not-so-obvious as well as the obvious." It'll save you a world of pain.

Part I

And, on that note: There are things in the arts, as there are things in life, that you will not like to do because they may feel tedious or pedantic. However, tedious and pedantic are a part of life; they come with the territory and are at times a necessary evil. So, find a way to get through it because it is worth the payoff.

Mars and Venus in Music

(Males and Females)

Mars and Venus

I am in the minority in a predominantly female occupation. As a student, I was also a minority as a young man and therefore studied mostly with women, with the exception of one male teacher. This, of course, had its advantages and disadvantages. I've been able to weed out these disadvantages by simply teaching and rediscovering how things work from the ground floor up. Because of this state of affairs, I am a big proponent on voice being tag-team taught by both a man and a woman—though most couldn't afford it, it is nice in theory. And because I've been inundated with female students (I'd say two-thirds), I've had to become really good at troubleshooting the female voice. The female voice can do many things. I believe much more is expected from the female voice than males, as if bearing children weren't enough. Sorry, ladies.

That said, one thing that has become plain to me is that men and women are different. I hope you were sitting down for that one. I've come to see that what works for the female does not always work for the male, and vice versa. For example: the vowel sound *i* (as in *bee*) in a man's mouth usually doesn't feel like there is enough space; in fact, it can feel downright lousy. However, the vowel sound *a* (as in *far*) will feel like home. For women, *a* (as in *far*) can feel swallowed, falling in the back, where *i* (as in *bee*) feels like home. Conversely, *a* becomes a challenge for women to overcome, and *i* for men. There are always exceptions, of course, but generally speaking I have found this to be true. And since men are from M(A)RS and women are from V(E)NUS, I felt it was important to differentiate between the two; however, ladies first.

(Vowels in italic as shown in the International Phonetic Alphabet)

Colors of Sound

Because most of us learn by imitation, the need for theory and finding your authentic sound becomes paramount in a lesson. It's like learning to play the piano or guitar by ear for years and suddenly being asked to read music. There is a tremendous gap between the two. The task becomes identifying what sounds you're making. For example, there are a number of different sounds the female voice can make: head voice, chest or chest belt, mixed voice, and high mixed belt. Most females we listen to are doing one, two, or all of the above. We get to sit back and enjoy the many colors of their sounds. But let me go ahead and break each one down.

Head Voice

This is a sound that resonates in the skull, an ethereal ring of sound that spins way up into the stratosphere. Think Julie Andrews, Audra McDonald, Kristin Chenoweth. Not to say that these women do not employ other colors of sound on the palette, but what you hear predominantly when you listen to these women is that hoot-like head sound, also known as legit, classical, or soprano.

Chest Voice/Belt

This sound sits in the lower part of the register and body: chest cavity, neck, and mouth. It can be found in crooners, rock and pop, and country. Think Rosemary Clooney, Karen Carpenter, Carole King. When women give this resonance a "goose," they are chest belting, a sound heard in the golden era of musical theater. Think Liza Minnelli, Carol Burnett, Patti Lupone. In rock and pop, think Donna Summer, Linda Ronstadt, Bette Midler. In country, think Carrie Underwood, Reba McEntire, Patsy Cline. These are old-school belters who hit us with a sound that ignites us to leap out of the very chairs we are sitting upon.

Un-bridged: The two shall not meet

Women who travel between these two sounds without having a connection or bridge can be found in pop, folk, and folk rock. Think Joni Mitchell, Carly Simon, Jewel; there is a distinct difference between the two sounds, making it yodel-like.

Mixed Voice

Those who have worked at building a connection between the two, called a mix, can be found in many arenas of music, most definitely in classical and musical theater, a more trained sound. But it can be found in other arenas. In rock, think Kelly Clarkson. In musical theater, think Barbara Cook. In the pop world, think Barbra Streisand.

High Mixed Belt

This sound is basically a belt on high. It can be found in contemporary musical theater. Think Sherie Rene Scott, Laura Bell Bundy. In rock, both old-school and new, think Janis Joplin, Christina Aguilera. In R&B, think Patti LaBelle and Aretha Franklin. In pop, think Celine Dion, Whitney Houston, and Mariah Carey. This sound so has the pedal to the metal; where a chest belt goes about sixty to sixty-five miles an hour, this sound passes it by in the left lane doing an easy eighty-five. For me, the difference between the two is that although they can both raise the hair on your arms and send chills down your back, the chest belt has more of a warmth, where the high mixed belt has a sense of being suspended in air without a net.

In conclusion, the fun and play that women have with these various mixes and belts is that they can choose according to the moment in a piece of music just how much chest or head they're going to give it, making the ratio between the two a constantly changing thing. Women with a more classical training will often have more head in their mix, whereas others will always be more chest dominant. Once a female's ducks are lined up in a row, then this kind of play can be had, and the fun begins. Listen for these colors of sound when going back to your favorite female singers. This is where making music becomes paramount. That's why we train, so that we can execute whatever we hear in the moment—complete freedom to express soul and emotion while making music, beauty, and fun.

Masculinity and the Male Voice

Not until recently did men make up one-third of my student base. Something's changing. Men are catching the wave that perhaps it is not only cool to sing but to study as well, something that the likes of Sinatra, Elvis, and Bono have helped to influence in this patriarchal culture of ours—much the way the Food Network has made cooking an acceptable and cool thing for men, with the likes of Bobby Flay, Emeril Lagasse, and many others.

Part I

Bridge

The two shall meet. There is one thing in common that all voices have, men and women: the need to learn how to bridge it from bottom to top. The middle of the voice is a tricky place. And that really becomes the bulk of the work for me, teaching young singers how to do this without pushing and hurting themselves. Men have to learn how to smoothly go from their chest voices up through the middle, which resonates in the mouth, to the nasal resonator, especially tenors. Most will push to do this, some figure it out on their own, and some just do it naturally but then have to learn just exactly what it is they are doing for technique's sake. There are terms still being used for men, like head voice and belt, that just never feel right to me, although I use them for the sake of clarity. And, sure, it's just a matter of semantics, but I still think there should be new terms for men's voices. Albeit, since there aren't any universally, I will use the same old hackneyed terms that we use for women, with a few creative turns of my own.

Crooners

When we're talking about men like Sinatra, Bing Crosby, Tony Bennett, and hundreds of others, men who sang from "The Great American Songbook," we are talking about crooners. What makes these voices exciting is the fact that what these men often do is belt it out. Belting feels like yelling and sounds like yelling "prettily." It's powerful to do, and it is powerful to listen to. When you're listening to a guy like Tony Bennett, you are hearing a much higher range, that of a tenor—he belts up to the stratosphere, and still does by the way, as opposed to Sinatra, who was always more of a high baritone. Sinatra had those higher notes that he could visit, belt out, and leave, whereas Bennett lives there. Bennett, to me, also has a much more classically trained sound in his voice, like Vic Damone and Jack Jones. And Bennett has even talked about studying what is known as bel canto, which might explain why the guy can still sing like a forty-year-old. He is in his eighties, quite a model to study for longevity. But despite this classical sound, he knows how to swing, just like Sinatra, hands down. Other guys who had a huge range and could belt it out of the ballpark are Sammy Davis Jr. and Mel Tormé. Sammy Davis Jr. could sing anyone out of the room as well as dance his ass off and do incredible impressions. Mel Tormé, who you can also find in the jazz world, was a world-class musician, composer, and singer and scatted like no one's business. And as far as belting it out goes, it doesn't get any better than Mel or Sammy. Lighter crooners, like Bing Crosby, guys who kept it pretty steady, even, and never blasted are Nat King Cole and Dean Martin. These are beautiful, mellow voices. Men who came later on and continued the tradition of crooning were, Bobby Darin, Andy Williams, Engelbert Humperdinck, and Tom Jones.

Falsetto, Doo-Wop, and Rock and Roll

When a boy's voice changes, they say it takes about three years for it to settle. The voice drops an octave, whereas the female voice only drops a tone or two, a minimal change. But that soprano range that a boy once had is now gone as he cracks and yodels in a completely new place, making the soprano range unobtainable for a while, as the voice is learning and taking some time to settle. It is a tremendous physical and hormonal change, as well as vocal. They say that during this spurt, the larynx grows by 60 percent, along with a significant growth in the facial bones, as the voice drops into the basement called the chest.

Some, for a while, can have a difficult time matching pitch as well. This happened to me when my voice changed. I thought I would never be able to sing again. In my research about this, I've learned that this change is completely involuntary and has nothing to do with the ear. I have on one occasion worked with a young boy who had this problem and eventually helped him to match pitch again. It is a relearning of muscular coordination with a little bit of patience, understanding, and encouragement. When the dust has settled, a young man can again find this higher register once known as soprano, now known as falsetto, through breath and training, or he will most likely just try to push to get up there. At the time my friend encouraged me to work with her voice teacher, I was doing the same. I eventually was able to get up there more easily with her help, using scales, breath, repertoire, and practice.

The falsetto wasn't in the ear of the culture until the 1950s rolled around with doo-wop and groups like Frankie Valli and The Four Seasons. Guys were now ascending up into their upper registers in a more whiny sound that became popular and acceptable, as opposed to the brassier belt of Sinatra, Crosby, and Bennett, while Elvis, a game changer, a pioneer who brought along his uncontrollable pelvic region that would change the face of popular music forever, did not show off his falsetto. He kept it at home while he growled, belted it out, and made girls unconscious instead. Not bad, Elvis.

With the advent of rock and roll—you know, the devil's music—it moved from the whiny falsetto to a mix of the crooner belt and the latter. Sometimes it was just plain screaming; think the Beatles' "I Wanna Hold Your Hand," The Rolling Stones' "I Can't Get No Satisfaction," and so on. But as music moved into the 1970s, that same high yell turned sometimes into a thicker, passionate cry from voices like Thomas Clayton Powell of Blood, Sweat & Tears, Chicago, Billy Joel, and Elton John, while we also heard the mellow folk rock voices of James Taylor, Jim Croce, Harry Chapin, Gordon Lightfoot, and the Eagles. There are exceptional voices of this time, like Harry Nilsson who had an extraordinary range and could convey emotion up and down it. Art Garfunkel also had a fluid range both vocally and emotionally, expressing great depths of beauty and cries of passion.

This cry of passion that I refer to that has its roots in the crooner's belt would only up the ante through the seventies into the eighties with artists like Steve Perry of Journey, Freddie Mercury of Queen, Steven Tyler of Aerosmith, and many, many others—a thicker cry of passion. These men exhibit a phenomenon in their voices that I wouldn't recommend trying at home. Let it also be understood that most of them have probably trained and trained classically in order to handle the rigors of such acrobatic singing. (More on classical to come.)

I think with the advent of metal, this sound was layered once again. We are hearing it today with a voice like Dave Grohl's of the Foo Fighters; this sound is not a whine or a belt or a cry, it's a roar, very similar to what we hear James Hetfield, of Metallica, do. Again, kids, don't try this at home, unless you are naturally inclined to do so; then do me a favor, and go get some training.

Part I

The important thing for men is to make a smooth connection from the bottom of the voice through the middle and up into the new soprano or falsetto (which is called the break or passaggio, aka the passage), so that whatever you wind up doing, whether it is classical, belt, whine, cry, or roar, you can do it over and over and over again, having the kind of longevity that our friend Tony Bennett still exhibits.

Musical Theater, Classical Singing, and the Fear of Opera

When I first studied, I worked on Italian art songs, arias, and classical musical theater repertoire like that of Rogers and Hammerstein's *Carousel*. I wasn't interested in pursuing a classical career as a singer, but I enjoyed working on these pieces and the challenges they presented. Years later I went on to study Puccini, Mozart, and other classical repertoire of musical theater, like Leonard Bernstein's *West Side Story*, not easy. This music is glorious and absolutely the hardest stuff anyone will ever come across, certainly for me. However, even though I began to excel at this music, I still had no desire to pursue it professionally. The closest I came professionally was light opera. This is the music of Gilbert and Sullivan, Franz Lehár, and Jerome Kern to name a few: *The Pirates of Penzance*, *The Merry Widow*, and *Show Boat*, respectively. In fact my first professional job in New York City was with an Off-Broadway company called, The Light Opera of Manhattan (LOOM), where I got to be a part of some of these classic shows. LOOM was a repertory company that performed fifty-two weeks a year. We would perform one show while rehearsing another. This was a tremendous learning experience of old-school proportions. If available, I highly recommend it...once.

Here's my theory that I share with many: much like an actor who stretches his or her muscles working on Shakespeare, Ibsen, and Shaw (classical repertoire) who can then go on to more contemporary repertoire with greater ease because of this training, so it is with singers and musicians. In fact, for women it can only improve their belt, also making it easier. Men will also find greater ease, much like the rockers mentioned earlier who can wail. Men with a more classical sound in the golden age of Broadway musicals: Gordon MacRae, John Raitt, and John Cullum. Women with a more classical sound: Barbara Cook, Anna Maria Alberghetti, and Kelli O'Hara. Female opera singers: Dawn Upshaw, Renee Fleming, and Cecilia Bartoli. Male opera singers: Luciano Pavarotti, Placido Domingo, and Thomas Hampson.

Exposure to other kinds of music that are not your preference can hold a lot of surprises: you might find you like it, you might even jump on its band wagon, or you might just get great growth and pleasure from it, as I know I have.

The Arch of a Song
Acting in Music

The Arch of a Song: Acting in Music

Each song has an arch: a beginning, middle, and end. Each song is a little play, a small piece of theater. It tells a story, conveys feelings, and reveals character, relationship, a desire, and a conflict—all the elements of good drama, even the simplest ones.

When you're working on pieces from musical theater, everything is built in for you because each song should propel the story line. When you're singing pop music, especially contemporary pop, you may have to use your imagination a little more, but since the majority of pop music has been about "amour," I have broken it down into three universal aspects:

- I want you. Don't you want me, too?
- I got you, and you're all I'll ever need.
- I lost you, and I've got to get you back.

In the last fifty years, popular music has expanded its subjects from love to war and politics, drugs, familial relationships, and so on. Numerous artists, from the Beatles to Billy Joel, have written about these other aspects of life. We've come a long way from Gershwin's "I've Got a Crush on You" and the Beatles' "I Wanna Hold Your Hand." Crosby, Stills & Nash sang about the future generation with "Teach Your Children Well," Aretha Franklin sang for the women of her time with "R.E.S.P.E.C.T.," Billy Joel sang about the history of the world with "We Didn't Start the Fire," and Harry Chapin sang about father and son with "Cat's in the Cradle."

I think there are two distinctions to make in approaching the acting of a song. There is the kind where a singer stands in front of the microphone and conveys how he or she feels, having a certain connection to the music, and there is the kind where a singer conveys a song in a more specific way, which I call "acting in music." Neither one is the "correct" way; they are just different approaches, garnering different effects. Honestly, I wouldn't want to go to a rock concert and watch Aerosmith act a song. Follow? I'd want to see and hear them do what they do. But I'm going to talk more in detail about the latter approach in steps.

Bass Line

A lot can be derived based on the bass line of a piece, its tempo, and rhythm, even before you take a hard look at the lyrics. This cannot only be used for popular music but also musical theater repertoire as well. The writer is telling us much if it is well written. Is the bass line agitated, like in Sondheim's "Sweeney Todd"? Does it have an edgy, relentless eighth-note pulse like you find in Green Day's music? This is the stuff that you can get into your body, beginning with a more visceral experience. Music makes us move. It makes us feel. Is it a waltz, like the Rogers and Hammerstein piece, "Ten Minutes Ago," from *Cinderella*? When you do a waltz, it tells your body things. It's proper. It's sophisticated. It's held in and moves upward. This can give you a lot in figuring out who this character is and possibly what's going on by the physical feel it gives you. Cole Porter's "I Get a Kick Out of You," is more of a rumba or tango even. It is also sophisticated and classy but in a less proper manner than a waltz. It reeks of a party and sensuality while dressed in a gown or tux. If it's "Piece of My Heart" by Janis Joplin, it's the complete opposite. It's earthy, free, and wild, like Janis. If that doesn't do anything for you, then check your pulse to see if you're still alive. Whatever the bass line, let your body take the reigns while it informs the imagination.

Style

Another thing to look at is the year and period the song was written, and who wrote it. Also, what was the social climate? The answers to some of these questions will give you clues as to the core of the piece you are working on. If it's a piece from the 1970s by James Taylor, like "Fire and Rain," then the style of the song is soft, and easy, but the story is melancholy. This type of song was part of the folk rock explosion that got its start in the 1960s: peace, love, and rock and roll. That alone is worth volumes of acting work. "I Get a Kick Out of You," written by Mr. Porter in the 1930s, was published after the Great Depression and Prohibition, so looking into the history before its time, as well, can tell you much. This piece, which was first put into a movie, then later into a show called *Anything Goes*, is part of "The Great American Songbook," along with many other greats by the likes of the Gershwin Brothers, and Irving Berlin, all from the lower east side of Manhattan, while Porter was from London. That should give you a clue in distinction. Studying these songs, the writers, the artists, the history, the social climate, can inform you, and it can also be great learning about other times, worlds, and life experiences, making for a richer performance and a richer life.

Lyrics

Then we move to what the writer is telling us in the words: the story, the desire, the conflict, the character, the relationship. Sometimes the words can be in contrast to the bass line, or vice versa. Let's go back to "I Get a Kick Out of You." First off, it's got a smooth, swaying, martini-sipping bass line. It has that air of sophistication, a social feel like a party in The Hamptons. Makes me want to wear a tux. With that in mind, let's look at the lyrics in the chorus of the song, also known as the hook.

> *"I get no kick from champagne,*
> *Mere alcohol doesn't thrill me at all,*
> *So tell me why should it be true.*
> *That I get a kick out of you?*

This person is perplexed. He's posing a question. How can this someone be trumping champagne and booze? Who are you, and why are you doing this to me? He even goes on later in the song to say:

> *"Flying too high with some gal in the sky*
> *Is my idea of nothing to do.*
> *Yet I get a kick out of you."*

So, I think it's fair to say that this person is someone of privilege, rich perhaps, but terribly, terribly bored. But now comes this someone who's knocking him off his feet and throwing him for a loop. Let's look at the bridge:

> *"I get a kick every time I see you're standing*
> *there before me.*
> *I get a kick tho' it's clear to see*
> *You obviously don't adore me."*

Conflict. You've got a bass line that is saying, "This is a party, look at me I'm swaying, I'm in a tux," but the lyrics are saying something else. This person...doesn't want me. This contrast supplies tension. When we have two opposing forces, we have everything we need as actors: conflict. The body is saying one thing while the voice is saying another.

Now, let's go to the very beginning of the song and look at the verse.

> *"My story is much too sad to be told,*
> *But practically everything leaves me totally cold.*
> *The only exception I know is the case,*
> *When I'm out on a quiet spree,*
> *Fighting vainly the old ennui,*
> *And I suddenly turn and see-your fabulous face."*

People who are indulged can become bored, numb, or, in this case, cold. The Beatles were right: money can't buy you love. This gives people character, where they've been, what happened to them, and where they are now because of it. Then along comes someone who sets their hearts on fire, but, alas, the person is not interested. So, you've got character, desire or want, relationship, about whom they're singing, and conflict. Now, how does one put this all together in the arch of a song?

Impetus

What catapults singers into songs besides the fact that after the introduction they're supposed to sing? It's not enough. If you're going to take this approach, you must find a reason to sing. Starting is always the hardest part. Things often begin where they end. You will see this in life as well. After all, most art is just imitating life. So, often I look at what happens near the end of the piece, because it often explains why people speak in the first place. At the end of the bridge, we find out that the person they desire does not return the favor: conflict. This conflict becomes the impetus to sing. I want you. Don't you want me, too? Or, in this case, why don't you want me, too?

Action

If up until now, almost everything left me cold and now this comes along and sets my heart on fire, you better believe I'd do whatever it took to get more of that no matter what the circumstance. Alas, there is a conflict. The person he desires does not return the favor. What do people do when they can't get what they want? They hope. They try a different route. And when that doesn't work, they try another one. If this song falls under the "I want you. Don't you want me too?" category, then, man, you'd better want it.

So, now...action. Maybe I'm putting on my best tux to get their attention. You know, I clean up good, or so I've been told. Perhaps I'm going to get myself good and drunk and lament in the moonlight while I figure out a way to get to her. So, I'm plotting with booze in a tux. Maybe I'm daydreaming. Catching my drift? The wanting what you can't have is the impetus, the thing that catapults you into the song. The rest is how you're going to get it—the action—without ever knowing the outcome, like real life.

Here's the breakdown of the song we derived from the bass line, style, and lyrics:

Impetus, the reason to sing: You make me feel alive, warm, and hot for the very first time when all else has left me cold. I must have you.

Character, who you are: Privileged, cold, and empty, but now hopeful.

Relationship, who you are singing to or about: A man or woman who is turning up your thermostat.

Desire, what you want: To feel alive and in love.

Conflict, what's getting in the way: He or she doesn't want me the way I want him or her.

Action, what I'm doing about it: Trying on a new dress or tux, lamenting in the moonlight, drinking, plotting, all of the above.

Imagination, the most important element: Allow the tools to open up your imagination and let it run wild. This work will inform your vocals in a way that you could never have consciously derived by playing vocal tricks and crafting merely by your ear. It will become a buffer, taking away self-consciousness by driving you into the moment, deeper and deeper as it goes. And, man, is it fun.

In Conclusion: Think Less, Feel More—A Paradox

At a certain juncture in my acting training, the teacher would say: "Now forget about all the work and just be," this after weeks of toiling blood, sweat, and tears to nail each moment. With no idea of how to wrap my tired, worn-out brain around such a concept, I would try to do what the teacher told me. In retrospect, the reason why I was so unable to comprehend this was because what the teacher was putting forth was a paradox. A paradox is something that may seem contradictory or illogical, incongruous, but is somehow true. One of those life things you can't really explain, like loving someone while simultaneously disliking them intensely. Incongruous? Absolutely, but not impossible.

After a good number of years training as a singer, I had a breakthrough one day. After I'd gotten through what had been a very difficult and back-breaking piece with great ease, I remarked at this, as if I'd been doing nothing. To which my teacher shouted, "When it's right, it feels effortless." Can't tell you how many backflips my brain did after hearing that statement. Again with the paradoxes!

How many of us have watched experts in their fields do what they do, such as athletes, dancers, and Olympians, and remarked at how easy they made it look, followed by disastrous attempts at trying it ourselves and finding out how incredibly difficult it was? Anything executed with the appearance of great effortlessness took great effort to get there. What I felt that day at my voice lesson was the absence of effort. And the reason I had arrived at that point was because of the very effort I had put into it. What a payoff. When the acting teacher told us to "forget the work," he was telling us to stop thinking so hard and trust that the work we'd done was there. After all is said and done and you have applied everything you know to do as a singer, forget the work: think less, and feel more.

Part II:
Learning, Teaching, and Culture

Part II
Learning, Techniques, and Culture

Studying: How We Learn

Patience, Process, Discipline, and Practice

Do all good things come to those who wait? Who the hell knows. But, patience is a number one requirement when it comes to growth in training. Some want it *today*. Others want it *yesterday*. I'll tell ya this much, today's technology and the generations being raised on it are in for some rude awakenings. And as far as auto-tune goes, I say, learn how to sing on pitch at all times. Be that good. If a famous singer uses it in concerts because of the fatigue that sets in due to the grueling nature of touring, fine. People pay a lot to see those performers, and since it's available, why not? But for the rest of you, learn how to do this thing right. When you become famous, then auto-tune away.

This is a process. And here are some synonyms of "process" to chew on: way, means, mode, method, system, usage, procedure, step, line of action, the way of, the how.

The how. This is what we're looking for: how. How do I do this well?

That's the question. That's what leads all of us into training, whatever kind it may be. We look for a teacher to teach and guide us to the "how to." In the singer's tool bag, I talked about the tools that one would be using to unlock the voice and make it better. But now I want to talk about this process of learning and getting there. It is often the getting there in life that is always more interesting than the destination, although we are culturally obsessed with results. And again I say patience, my child. The getting there can be interesting, fascinating, strewn with volumes of learning, and fun.

When I was studying, the pattern went something like this; I'd go to lessons, start to work with the scales and pieces given to me by my teacher. I'd work with the recording of the lesson through the week. Sometimes I'd just listen to the recording. I found this aspect incredibly helpful and instructive. Then when I went to practice, it was your basic trial and error. Then, back to lessons I'd go, try out what I had practiced at home, and see if I had done anything right. And then home again. And this would layer and layer and layer, week in, week out. I also found that sometimes taking some time off helped enormously. In doing this, I learned inadvertently that it gave me time to digest the tremendous amount of information I was taking in every week. Remember, there is only so much that we can take in. Imagine eating a whole steak in one sitting, chewing a bit but not swallowing it all. Like food, information must be chewed, and chewed down to little bits so that it can be swallowed and digested. Over time, I got better because I showed up, and I took time during the week to practice.

We grow by receiving good, solid instruction, then we practice by having discipline; we go through our drills or scales, and over time this will make us fit, proficient, or conditioned.

Part II

When I was growing up, I had parents who required me to practice my musical instruments every day. Did I want to? Hell, no! Am I glad they made me? Hell, yes. Any form of practice that we do when we're younger instills in us varying amounts of discipline, which I'm sorry to say is going to be harder to find when you're older. So, kids who excelled in schoolwork, athletics, music, drama, etc., have a certain amount of that built into their cells that they can call upon later in life. It's integral. As a teacher, I discovered that the most disciplined students I encountered were dancers and still are. I quickly became enamored with their work ethic. From a very early age, most dancers are in class every day after school, much in the way children train for the Olympics. These and these only are the students who I admonish at times to take a night off and eat a bag of potato chips, because there's discipline, and then there's overkill. But for the rest of us, back to work.

As far as lessons go, you have to show up every week, on time. And when you're at the lesson, you have to be in the lesson. Be in each moment with the teacher, or you're wasting your time, money, and the energy of the teacher. Which brings me to an important aspect of the relationship between a teacher and a student in a private voice lesson setting. Sometimes we think we know what a teacher is talking about, and sometimes we just act like we do. I was one of those students who wanted to impress the teachers, so I made like I understood everything they said—until one day when I realized I wasn't learning much, and it was time to start asking questions. And I'm glad I did. But that was an aspect of myself that I got to learn about and change.

I think things can get lost in the translation. Information is imparted; the student interprets it in her center of reference, drawing his or her own conclusions, but is it what the teacher intended? This is the kind of thing that goes on between human beings all the time in conversation. Someone says something, we interpret, and a translation is made, right or wrong. If you feel that something is getting lost in translation, then it's time to get it clarified. If you're dealing with a teacher who doesn't liked to be asked a lot of questions, then I strongly suggest shopping for a new one. It's your money, your time, and your life. In saying this, I'm not trying to put anyone out of business, I'm just giving you the right to know that it's okay to move on and go where you're getting what you need.

Now, a word about where to practice: It is not easy for any musician to find a place to practice, where she won't be hearing an endless barrage of family and neighbors banging on walls, yelling, "Knock it off!" A band or orchestra can warm up in a rehearsal room collectively before a concert. Garage bands can make enough volume worthy of going off the decibel charts and be considered cool, but singers? Singers warming up is *not* cool. Singers are banned to closets, street corners, and subway platforms so as not to disturb. It is not easy. I have warmed up in alleyways, bushes, bathroom stalls, church basements, automobiles, rooftops, and the woods—anywhere I could have a little privacy and not disturb. Truth is, no singer wants anyone to hear her warm up. A scale is not a song.

Rehearsal spaces can be rented, schedules with roommates and spouses can be arranged, and so on, so that a singer can find time to practice and warm up for an audition or gig. I have been fortunate to have had a few neighbors over the years who actually enjoyed my practice time and told me so. But it is not always like this. Another thing that can be looked into is soundproofing a decent-sized closet and making your own singing booth for practice. A pillow gently pressed against your mouth may not be preferable, but it can muffle a good amount of noise. Where there's a will, there's a way. Wherever you find your zone, make it yours and practice your heart out.

The Three *S*'s

Three things are key in the development of the singing voice: stretch, strength, and stamina. One must consciously train, that is to say, become aware of the "how to," in order to use his instrument in the most healthiest, efficient way possible without having to "think." This is also known as "muscle memory." When one can rely on this, then the fun begins, because a person is freed to make music as the body responds to what the ears hear, with all three *S*'s in motion: stretch, strength, and stamina.

Much of this work can be likened to the way a physical trainer works with a client, for what you are training when learning the voice is a constant coordination and strengthening of muscles, though one would never know it by the naked eye. Again, with the voice residing inside of the human being, the awesome mechanics of our anatomy go unseen. Sometimes upon leaving a lesson I'd felt as if I'd been to the gym, with the constant usage of muscles of the respiratory system being called upon and stretching my range. It's a workout, man.

Stretch, which can also be thought of as agility, is essential because in order to grow you must move past your comfort zone just a little. So, when I'm working with a student, much like a personal trainer, I may push them just a bit past their comfort zone by having them go up a half step higher in a scale than they had the week before. This of course is all based on what I'm hearing and seeing in the moment while making comparisons to past lessons. At first it may feel a little scary for the student, but if it's done slowly and wisely, they will over time, and pretty quickly, I might add, become comfortable with this new height. Honestly, I liken it to someone on a bench press doing one more rep than they're used to and doing with the safety and help of a spotter, someone stronger and more knowledgeable.

In weight training, strength is built by an ongoing discipline of regular routine workouts and a certain amount of reps per set. Like the guy who goes an extra rep in a set than he's used to, he will eventually be able to add another five or ten pounds to the bar because he has become conditioned to this new amount of weight. He's reached a new plateau, and he's gotten stronger. For the singer, strength comes with conditioning as well. He comes to get used to doing a certain routine of scales and in time gets better at them from the sheer repetition. Strength comes from the express desire to improve and the discipline and dedication that must follow in order to get the job done.

Strength, in time, makes for more strength. The stronger the singer becomes, the more he or she can endure. In opera, singers need tremendous stamina. Stamina is the ability to endure. But whatever the style, singers who are called upon to sing on a regular basis will need it. In fact, given that a singer has a good, solid technique, just using his or her instrument on a regular basis will build the very stamina they need. Broadway performers use their voices eight times a week. Opera singers sing huge amounts of rigorous music at least twice a week in performance. Pop and rock singers travel the world doing one-nighters. That takes stamina, baby.

Overthinking It

Imagine as you walk up a flight of stairs that you suddenly become compelled to think about the coordination of leg and torso muscles and how they enable you to get up that flight of stairs. Now, imagine trying to help them out by doing the thinking for them. You may wind up paralyzed on that staircase with a crew of angry pedestrians held up behind you. This is what it's like when we overthink things. Here's the thing. You will never get it "right" upon the first try. If you do, that's beginner's luck. If you don't, that's normal. When a teacher gives an instruction, hopefully she is not expecting you to "get it" immediately, nor should you be expected to. It's all food for thought. This is an organic process. Take what you've been instructed to do home with you—again, trial and error. Listen to the recording of your lesson. With each listen you may hear things you did not prior. Then try it. You'll get it in time. In the meantime, don't overanalyze. Take it in. Be a sponge. Soak it up, and do your best. This is how it works.

We've been so conditioned to not make mistakes that, I believe, this is why we overthink things. It's purely a survival mechanism. I've done it, too. And it takes time to trust someone to allow you to make a mistake. Then at home when there's no one there to judge you, and you still find yourself getting too inside your head over something, just open your mouth, take a breath, and sing. Try the very thing that your teacher is talking about. Take that in with you, and see how it goes.

And honestly, when things become frustrating during practice time, shut it down. Since *you* are the instrument, it'll never work to push through it, not effectively anyhow. When things got terribly frustrating for me, this is precisely what I did: shut it down. Try the couch; kick your feet up. I highly recommend it.

Pedagogy
How We Teach

Cracking: An Occupational Hazard

There are certain expectations for anyone who enters a voice lesson for the first time. There is fear of judgment. Singing is a vulnerable thing, because the voice is you. So there is apprehension. For at any given moment, the student who is singing may crack. And when one cracks, there is no "takie-backsies." It is now out there in the universe, embedded in the ears and memories of the listeners or, in this case, the so-called expert sitting behind the piano, collecting your check at the end of the lesson.

Think about famous singers who can never live down forgetting the lyrics to "The Star-Spangled Banner" or who sing a note or two flat or sharp. We don't exactly live in the most forgiving culture.

In my experience, when a student cracks, there is no amount of consolation I can give, as they are often inconsolable. However, the planet seems to continue to rotate, and life moves on. Anatomically speaking, cracking can be due to a lack of muscular coordination, breath, and placement that can be bettered with training, time, and practice.

No one wants to sound ugly. There are people who won't even sing "Happy Birthday" at a party for fear of public humiliation—and who could blame them? Everyone wants to make a good first impression. Some come to a voice lesson with a good-sounding voice accompanied with a certain degree of confidence with the objective of improving what they already have. Some come with the delusion that they are the next Sinatra or Streisand, and everyone else comes somewhere in between. Whatever the case, it takes courage to show up because—let's be honest—if you don't sound like the guy on the record, then siddown and shut up, right?

I grew up with a certain amount of natural ability and therefore was encouraged by those around me to keep it up. Not all are so fortunate. Most come out of the womb singing, but it's not a matter of that, it's a matter of who wants to hear them. As I said, I had the encouragement of family, teachers, and peers that gave me the right to be heard and a fair amount of confidence to do so. It subsequently paved the way for me to seek improvement as well.

Music saved me as a child. I believe it can give relief as well as inspiration. It can soothe one's soul. So, to take that from someone early on is a great disservice. I feel that one of the things I've done as a voice teacher is to restore that back to the student through singing. Here are some other things that I believe making music can bring:

- Fun
- Relaxation
- Expression
- Joy
- Passion
- A way to get stale air out of the lungs and fresh air back in
- A release of tension
- An adrenaline high
- Comfort
- A way to make yourself happy
- A thrill
- A way to be in the moment
- A way to de-stress and just forget about life

Training accompanied with practice can lead to security and confidence to help a person trust that what comes out of one's mouth will be pleasing to a room full of anxious listeners. And those listening may also receive the benefits listed above just by one's passing along the gift of music, which happens to be his voice.

To Critique or Nurture? That Is the Question

I feel that criticism is highly overrated. If I'm not criticizing a student, am I really doing my job? It's a question I've come face-to-face with. I looked it up in the dictionary, and here's what I found:

Criticism: The act of criticizing usually unfavorably.

Critique: Evaluate. To find fault with. Point out the faults of.

Unfavorable? Point out the faults of? I don't know about you, but guess what I walk away with if all a teacher does is criticize me?

Criticism...unfavorable, negative criticism. It's really no different than feeling more tension when someone tells you to relax! Here's more from Mr. Webster:

Nurture: Training. Suckle. To provide. Nourishment. Food.

I have often thought of nurturing as a dominantly feminine characteristic. But after reading that definition, I began to think differently. It reminded me of what it must take to raise a child. But doesn't it take both a gentle and firm hand to properly bring one up? So, could nurture be both a feminine and masculine trait? After all, Webster used the word *training* to define nurture. It's actually the first word used here. Then comes suckle. We have traditionally looked at criticism as a masculine trait and nurture as a feminine one. Perhaps it's both.

Here are my questions: What good does it do a student to find unfavorableness with him or her? How is that helpful? Over the years, I found a way of dealing with this issue. If in the moment I could not find a way to help a student out of an unuseful habit, I would wait until I could. I mean, what's the point of telling someone, "You sing with too much tension" or "Stand up straight"? As far as I'm concerned, the man on the street can now tell you if you're "pitchy," thanks to *American Idol*, so what good am I if I do the same? From my own experience and talks with students, I've concluded that if all you're getting from someone is criticism, you are leaving him or her with one question and one question only: how do I fix it? And you are leaving a student with one feeling and one feeling only: discouragement.

We are living in an age where we see more criticism and judgment than ever before. Entertainment shows are dominated with a panel of judges waxing on in their critiques as America fumbles for their cell phones to "vote their favorite singer." Or, we are hearing the same three judges give praise worthy of a case of diabetes. Too much. Where's the balance? What a student needs is a sugar-free blend of nurture and criticism. Or how about a strict diet of nourishment? To nurture or to criticize? Yes, that is the question, Hamlet. Perhaps it is both: a gentle but firm hand, a teacher who waits to speak until he knows how to correct the unfavorableness he is seeing in the student, a teacher who leaves the student with a way to fix things and a feeling that he or she will eventually be able to get there. Hope rather than defeat.

Too Much Talking

My very first teacher, Myra, a sassy broad, sat behind her baby grand playing scales and sipping hot water with lemon all the day long as she grew rich off teaching all the eager high school kids in the neighborhood. I was seventeen at the time. I remember that she was an avid fan of basketball. When asked why, she'd reply, "Because it's sooo exciting!" I didn't share her enthusiasm, but I appreciated her love for it. And besides the scales and songs we worked on, that is what I primarily remember about her.

When I first started teaching, I regarded her and those lessons as too simple, while I waxed on and on about the technique of singing. But when you start to become aware of your students' eyes glazing over on more than one occasion, it might be time for a reevaluation.

Myra gave all her students the same basic scale set. We showed up, we went through them, and then we worked on anything from an Italian art song to Rogers and Hammerstein. As long as I practiced those scales and worked on those songs, I got better. Simple. I showed up. I practiced. I improved. Sometimes as I got better, she'd throw a new scale at me, something to challenge and keep my interest and antennae up. But, there were no long dissertations or drawn-out explanations on the voice. It's funny how our teachers become so much smarter as we get older.

I think there is a time for talk, of course. There is a time for everything: turn, turn, turn. But sometimes... sometimes, it is enough to simply open up your mouth, take a breath, and let the air and the words do the work. There is much to be learned in the doing. I'm not the only teacher in the room.

A Challenge, You Say?

Why must everything be a challenge? Why have we been taught that if you work on something that you like or comes naturally, it will be a waste of time? This is a pervasive piece in our educational think tank: fun equals unproductivity, and a non-challenge equals weakness. But, who's to say that working on something that you like implies an absence of a challenge? I beg to differ. Most students come to voice lessons, chomping at the bit to work on a plethora of repertoire. I most certainly did. That doesn't mean that the voice teacher will be thrilled with everything the student desires to sing, just as the student will not be thrilled with the suggestions made by the teacher. In other words, there is a good amount of eye rolling on behalf of both. I have run the gamut. I have taught with an agenda, and I have relinquished it as well. In other words, I have both suggested pieces to students and allowed them to choose their own. Inevitably, I have found a balance of the two works best. I'm a great believer in this: singing material that a student likes will do much for their growth, because unlike something that is forced upon them, they will be more receptive to learning because of this express desire to communicate their chosen piece. In time, when they begin to trust me, I will assign them pieces for their furthered growth. Then when they go back to pieces they desire, they will bring to them the technique learned from the pieces I once suggested. What a beautiful cycle.

Often students will want to do a piece that is out of their league. This is very common. This happens for a couple of reasons: one, they want to recreate the surge of power they felt when they first heard it done by the original artist, and two, they want to prove to themselves that they can do it as well. As a student, I was no different. As a teacher, I advise them that they are not ready to take on the challenge without discouragement, or I allow it, but transpose it down to a more comfortable key. With the latter choice herein lies the rub: students perceive transpositions as a weakness, a feeling of inadequacy. A big aspect of my training was bringing pieces down if not in its entirety, at least the more difficult sections. Less challenging? No way. More accessible? You bet. Also, for some unknown reason, many pieces of popular music are published in the most ridiculously high keys, keys that professionals wouldn't even waste their time with, and I make sure my students know this. Once a student acquiesces to work on the piece in a lowered key, they quickly forget the inadequacy they once felt because of the ability they now find in singing the piece they've been dreaming of. In time because of the relaxation that ensues, they are able to bring it up to the original key, as was my experience as a student. Novice mountain climbers don't hit Everest first. However, whatever lesser mountains they wind up on, there is great learning and sheer joy in the climbing.

A New School of Thought

There's an old school of thought that goes: "Break you down to build you back up." In other words, break down your defenses in order to start you from scratch, a clean slate, and build from the ground floor up. Quite a lofty notion, I think. Well meant, but presumptuous, irresponsible, and dangerous. Not to mention the unequal balance between the breaking down and the building back up, often, in my experience, leaning more toward the breaking down.

I don't know about anyone else, but when I arrived on the scene, I was about as broken down as I could get. If students enter with a cocky, know-it-all attitude, they will find out soon enough they don't know much. Besides, arrogance is only the B side of fear. If a teacher with a gentle but firm hand earns their trust, the defenses will drop and open up a vat for knowledge and learning.

It's time for a new school of thought. And we don't have to throw the baby out with the bathwater. If it worked then and it works now, I keep it. If it doesn't, it goes out with the bucket of dirty water. If I don't do this, then I am perpetuating an old-school model. And if the old-school model isn't working, then nothing's going to get any better. This way of thinking keeps me in the moment. Tradition may be a nice thing, a nice sentiment, but it can also be stale, rigid, and unproductive. Teaching keeps me in the moment because it constantly forces me to flex my muscles. And when I do this, I learn, too.

Also, the greatest lessons I have learned, I have learned because of my students. If I listen to them, whatever it may be, then I can reexamine, rearticulate, go back to the drawing board, and come back in time with a new way of looking at things. Also, if I listen to them, then my job actually becomes easier. I don't have to have all the answers. They help me to find them, whether they know it or not. One cannot teach in a vacuum. There are two human beings in that room. There is a conversation with room for growth and new ideas. Together, you can change the way we teach and the way we learn, making a new model.

A Culture of Singing

Belting, Broadway Musicals, and the Men Who Write Them

When young women come to me, they either have been belting from out of the womb or were discouraged from doing it. The discouragement usually comes from a well-intentioned chorus teacher who does not want the child to hurt herself or from a culture that dictates women must only sing in their head voices and sound soft and pretty. Despite the warnings of the chorus teacher, many girls who are prone to yelling, or become cheerleaders, can wind up getting vocal nodules at an early age. Nodules, which are mostly diagnosed in women, are like a pair of blisters or callous-like lesions that lay on both vocal folds. (They normally come as a pair.) They can prevent women from singing higher up in their head resonance later on. Sometimes the nodules go away, sometimes they can live with them just fine, and sometimes they eventually have to get them removed. Whatever the case, if a female wants to belt, she eventually has to learn how to do it as healthily as possible.

The ones who were discouraged usually come to me terrified, with a chorus of monkeys on their backs, but soon come to find that they can do it without hurting themselves. In the beginning, they will feel like they are just yelling, but eventually they will get used to the sound and feel and love it. And the ones who've belted from out of the womb usually will learn that they've been doing it wrong by compromising their bodies in different ways. It usually takes some time to work out the old habits, but they too can learn how to do it more healthily and will attest that it feels so much better.

In teaching belt, I start with a piece from the golden era of musicals, when pieces were written in the female's natural chest belt range. Once they become more comfortable with this, they can move on to higher pieces that require a mixed belt range, bringing the head register along with the chest. As the music of Broadway moved into the pop sound of the late sixties and seventies, so did the style and ranges of what singers were being called upon to do. But the ante got upped as it moved into the late seventies and eighties with the British Invasion, and I'm not talking about the Fab Four. Women were now required to belt higher than was natural, what pedagogues of old would call a "registration violation." Corny, but true.

The 1970s of Broadway brought a genuine folk rock sound in keeping with the sounds of the radio by the likes of composers such as Marvin Hamlisch and Stephen Schwartz, while the Broadway musical theater sound of the forties and fifties was still kept alive by the likes of Kander and Ebb, Jerry Herman, and Stephen Sondheim. But with the advent of a little-known show called *Evita*, things would change for the female voice indefinitely.

Interestingly enough, Andrew Lloyd Webber, who wrote *Jesus Christ Superstar*, a rock opera, in the earlier seventies in keeping with the sounds of rock radio, would go on to write *Evita*, a pop opera, in the later seventies, that would begin to fuse a musical theater sound with a pop sound, making a new hybrid. Also interesting is that what *Jesus Christ Superstar* demanded of male singers now would shift to the female in *Evita*, a tall, tall order. When working on this repertoire with females, I have found that just by lowering it down a half step, it enables them to sing in a much more comfortable place. I have found this fact to be astounding. Astounding that Mr. Webber never got the memo. And the ball has been rolling ever since with shows such as *Next to Normal, Legally Blonde, Wicked*, and so on. Men have had greater demands put upon them as well with shows like *Rock of Ages, Next to Normal,* and *Miss Saigon*.

When a student realizes how difficult this repertoire is, I often say, "What do you expect? A man who doesn't sing for a living wrote it." Perhaps it would be nice if a composer put a little more thought into this fact that seems to be brushed aside on a regular basis. Perhaps with these greater demands in place, the eight-show-a-week schedule should be reevaluated. After all, what opera singer in her right mind would do more than one or two performances a week? It's no different with the rock opera, not to mention the dialogue, costume changes, and dance numbers to boot. The voice is you. It's a very small instrument, smaller than a piccolo. Yes, it can take a beating, but it's only human.

Can't Carry a Tune...

Early on in my teaching, I had a student who was tone deaf. Her only objective was to learn how to sing "Happy Birthday" on pitch. I understood the idea behind the goal. Those public situations can be every embarrassing. Unfortunately, I didn't know how to help someone with this problem. Albeit, I tried many different ways based on my instincts and knowledge of voice and music.

Someone who is tone deaf is often told early on by a parent, friend, or some authority figure like a teacher that he or she cannot sing. Subsequently, the person clams up from that moment and hardly ever utters another singing sound. When this happens, the person never gets any practice at how to use this organically given joy. I've come across students whose bodies seemed paralyzed when it came to singing, not having a clue of what it felt like—something the rest of us would take for granted like breathing. This is not natural. If you can make sound out of the womb, then you can sing. But as I said earlier, in our culture, it's not about that, it's about who wants to hear you. One guy I worked with wanted to learn how to sing on pitch so that he could serenade his girlfriend, a truly bittersweet situation. The maddening aspect was that his girlfriend, who was a "singer," would often tell him to stop when he did so. It was because of this aspect that this guy took on everything I gave him and worked as hard as he could, and so did I.

In helping these students, the best antidote I found was using my own voice as a guide as opposed to the piano. The timbre of the piano couldn't be further from the timbre of the human voice. In fact you'd be better off using a trombone or clarinet than a piano. And, quite naturally, what better way to match sound than with another human voice? Sometimes these things seem so obvious and simple that they are often overlooked. Also, any student who worked hard at it, both in and outside of the lesson, eventually came to sing on pitch and gained the confidence to do so. Where there's a will, there's a way. And anyone who finally learns how to sing on pitch is only coming back home.

Part II

In Closing: Serve the Music

Look, talent competitions have been around since dirt. And I'm pretty sure there's not a night where you can't find a singing competition on your television set. Singing competitions are just that: competitions. When competition gets ingrained in the arts, it is changing the nature of the beast. Business is business. But when their agenda is who can sing the loudest, nail the most melismata, and hold the longest note, then we lose something very vital—music. That these shows are adding new artists to the music industry is great. That they're giving opportunities to new and upcoming artists is wonderful. But let's not take the music out of the music. When I'm feeling nothing after a singer sings but how impressed I am by his or her talent, then something is wrong. Beautiful voices are a dime a dozen. Anyone can tell if you can sing well within a nanosecond of hearing you. Then we're looking for something more outside of the competitive arena. Hell, I've seen one of these shows where they put the singers in a boxing ring. What the hell does that have to do with music and the making of it? It doesn't. It's television.

I remember working as a waiter and listening to Billie Holiday as I would hang near the bar, waiting for the evening rush. As I did, I would cue in on her and be amazed at how all her feelings would pour out through each note she sang, and how I would feel them too. Talk about transcendent. And although very few can carry their emotion on the voice like that, it sure is something to aspire to—true authenticity. Singers of this era were a part of a more collaborative spirit. Although the singer stood in front of the band, it was an ensemble. She was only one part of a whole, not the whole.

The Intangible Singing Voice

When the competition is over and one singer sucker punches the other, it's time to get back to what it's really about, serving the music. And paradoxically, when a singer does that, the voice becomes even more impressive. And that, my friends, is a win-win.

Serve the music.

Appendix I: Health for the Singer

I remember coming back into show business after a brief hiatus in my mid to late twenties and being surrounded by a bunch of singers who in my estimation were tying themselves up in knots about what they could and couldn't do concerning the health and longevity of their voices. I've heard these laundry lists of dictates over the years ad nauseam. And although there are obvious things that are detrimental to the health of your voice, like smoking (not to mention every other vital organ), all other things in moderation, my friends. I've gathered the most talked about topics on health based on many a conversation with students in my studio and listed them here, plus recommendations to help along with each.

On Smoking

Telling anyone to not smoke because it's bad for them is like telling an alcoholic that drinking will kill them someday—they don't care. Smoking is an addiction like any other and, in some cases, worse than others. An addiction is a loss of control over a substance or behavior that puts the addict and others around them in harm's way. I know recovering alcoholics who attest to smoking being the harder habit of the two to quit. If you do smoke, hopefully you will come to yourself at some juncture and quit. When and if you do, there are many more aids out there to help you than there were years ago. Here are two:

www.nicodermcq.com
www.blucigs.com (Electronic cigarette. Not FDA approved)

On Coffee

Can coffee give you acid reflux? Sure, but so can tomatoes and spicy foods. If you have chronic heartburn and/or acid reflux, there are medicines and dietary changes out there to help, and, yes, you might have to give up coffee. It can be done. I've done it a number of different times in my life. Otherwise enjoy it, but don't drink it right before you sing.

On Mucus, Dryness, Hydration, and Moisture

Here's my theory: when we get dried out from cold weather, air conditioners, or overheated living spaces, our bodies go into overdrive and make an overabundance of mucus as a way to protect, hence the incessant clearing of our throats and singing through barricades of phlegm. We need mucus to live; it's a lubricant. Ideally, the vocal folds should have a thin layer of mucus covering them in order to work efficiently. Drinking water is important for hydration; however, too much of it can actually dry us out because it doesn't make moisture. Moisture is key. And when hydrating yourself before you sing, make sure you are not drinking water that is ice cold, but at a lukewarm temperature.

Dryness

I highly recommend buying yourself a good humidifier. You can find the no-fuss ones that only require filling them with water as opposed to having to buy filters and chemicals for keeping them clean. Once you find one,

Appendix I

turn that puppy on before you get ready for bed, so that you are receiving moisture all night long while you sleep instead of getting dried out.

Moisture

Glycerin is a key ingredient, as it makes moisture. I have found these products to be effective:

- Stoppers 4 Dry Mouth (mouth spray with glycerin), available at www.drugstore.com, www.Amazon.com, and www.Walgreens.com
- Grether's Pastilles: Lozenges are a singer's essential. Grether's Pastilles, available online and in drugstores, also contain glycerin and are available sugar-free.

Mucus

Mucinex is an expectorant and can be found also online or at most drug stores. This stuff really gets the mucus out and can also be found in generic form. Also the acidity in lemon juice will cut right through mucus. Squeeze a half of one into a glass of lukewarm water or a hot cup of tea.

On Sleep

You'd be amazed at how much lack of sleep or the right amount of sleep can affect the voice. It should no longer be a surprise. Knowing that the instrument is you, you also understand that how you treat your body will affect it. If you battle insomnia, I highly recommend melatonin (3–5 milligrams.) You may want to check with your doctor before doing so. Melatonin is natural and non-addictive. If your lifestyle is a busy one, and isn't allowing for sleep, figure out how to get a few naps in, especially if you're going to use your voice. The difference between a rested voice and an un-rested one is like night and day.

On Sore Throats

Very simply put, if you have a sore or strep throat, then you are dealing with swelling and should not be using it. The show must go on? I beg to differ. Stay off it if you want to "go on" and have a long career. I suggest these resources:

- **www.traditionalmedicinals.com: Their throat coat or** other herbal teas with a little honey work wonders to soothe the soreness.
- www.singerssavinggrace.com: This is a very helpful throat spray.

Also, I recommend going to your local Whole Foods or healthier grocery stores and investigating the world of throat sprays, as there are many. With these, you spray the back of your throat three times: once on the right side, once in the middle, and once on the left. Be sure to read the instructions before doing so.

Finally, take care of yourself, for you first. Don't expect others to pick up your slack. Then take care of yourself for your voice. You're the instrument. The voice is inside of you. You can't see or touch it, but you can take care of it and have it for your lifetime.

Appendix II: Styles of Sound— A Listening List

The following list is based on a number of sounds and artists that I discussed in the Venus and Mars chapter. Much can be garnered for technique by listening to what a singer is doing to suit their specific style of repertoire.

Under each style you'll see the following: a recommendation of artist(s), album titles, and tracks, concluding with a few comments and in some cases further recommendations of other artists.

This is fun homework, as all you have to do is open your ears while going in no particular order. Enjoy it.

A Preface

The artists listed here are in no way only capable of producing the one particular timbre that I've categorized them in. I've listed them in those particular categories because I feel they best represent them.

Belt/Musical Theater

Carol Burnett—*Once Upon a Mattress*: "The Swamps of Home," "Happily Ever After." Judy Holliday—*Bells Are Ringing*: "I'm Going Back." Angela Lansbury—*Mame*: "If He Walked into My Life," "Bosom Buddies" (with Beatrice Arthur). Patti LuPone—*Gypsy* (2008): "Everything's Coming up Roses." Liza Minnelli—*New York, New York*: "But The World Goes Round."

I chose these ladies of old-school chest belt because nary will you hear an ounce of head resonance. It's as if there is a bugle attached to their mouth, which is actually an accurate image for this style of sound: a coronet where there used to be a mouth. Also, listen for the incredible comedic timing of these ladies, and imagine what it must've been like to sit in a theater watching them. I did not include Ethel Merman, the queen of belt, in this category because although I'm sure many would disagree, in listening to her many recordings over the years, I hear a head resonance in her mix that I do not hear in the women I have recommended here. Nonetheless, if you want to hear quintessential Merman, listen to the original *Gypsy* Broadway soundtrack—powerful.

Belt/Pop-Rock—Female

Carole King—*Tapestry*: "(You Make Me Feel Like) A Natural Woman," "Home Again." Bette Midler—*The Divine Miss M*: "Friends." Also by her—*The Rose* (Original Soundtrack): "When a Man Loves a Woman." Linda Ronstadt—*Heart Like a Wheel*: "You're No Good," "When Will I Be Loved." Also by her—*Don't Cry Now*: "Desperado," "Love Has No Pride."

Some say belting is like yelling. I think this is valid to a degree. Also, I think that there are degrees of yelling in belt, for example, the high mixed belt, which is further down on this list. Again, there is a warmth to this sound as you listen to Linda, Bette, and Carole. With Bette there is a bit more yelling going on, especially on the selection from *The Rose*, but feel free to explore her body of work, as she has much depth of range. With Linda, there is no one who I have ever heard who belts with such fullness of sound. Check out her body of work, as she changed styles through the decades in order to stay current and employed, much the way Madonna changed hairstyles and wardrobe. Carole, although a little pinched at the top of her range, has incredible warmth to her earthy sounds, an earth mama who happens to write them all as well!

Others to listen to: Karen Carpenter (of The Carpenters), Donna Summer, Toni Tennille (of Captain & Tennille), and Melissa Manchester.

Belt/Pop-Rock—Male

David Clayton-Thomas (of Blood, Sweat & Tears)—*Blood, Sweat & Tears*: "And When I Die," "God Bless the Child." Billy Joel—*Piano Man*: "Captain Jack." Also by him—*Turnstiles*: "New York State of Mind." Elton John—*Goodbye Yellow Brick Road*: "Bennie and the Jets." Also by him—*Madman Across the Water*: "Levon."

Although as I've mentioned earlier in the book there should be a different term for men when it comes to "belting," that is precisely what these men do; they belt it out right out of the ballpark, home run. There is a total abandon present when these guys sing. They convey through their voices what singing should feel like: freedom and joy.

Classical—Soprano, Mezzo-Soprano, Tenor, Bass-Baritone (Respectively)

Dawn Upshaw—*Debussy: Forgotten Songs*: "Clair de Lune." Also by her—*I Wish it So*: "The Girls of Summer." Cecilia Bartoli—*The Vivaldi Album*: "Alma Oppressa."

Luciano Pavarotti *La Bohème* (Berlin Philharmonic): "Che Gelida Manina." Thomas Hampson—*The Very Best of Thomas Hampson*: "Largo Al Factotum" (*Il Barbiere di Siviglia,* Act 1). Also by him—*Leading Man/The Best of Broadway*: "Soliloquy" (*Carousel*).

I've listed here the usual suspects in voice type or range that you will find in classical repertoire as a starter. There is of course so much more to discover if interested. This sound requires a tremendous amount of space in one's mouth, particularly in the back or what is known as *loft* or *loft space*. It goes back to the vertical space that I spoke of in the Singer's Tool Bag section. Classical singing takes a tremendous amount of strength, agility, and musicianship. In the professional world, it requires a big voice in volume, as to be able to fill an opera house with it. In the case of Dawn Upshaw and Thomas Hampson, I've recommended other selections to exhibit how well they are able to cross over into other styles.

Classical Traditional Musical Theater—Female

Julie Andrews—*My Fair Lady*: "Just You Wait." Also by her—*The Sound of Music* (film soundtrack): "The Lonely Goatherd," "I Have Confidence." Kaye Ballard—*Carnival*: "Humming" (with Henry Lascoe). Barbara Cook—The Music Man: "My White Knight." Also by her—*Candide*: "Glitter and Be Gay." Madeline Kahn—*On the Twentieth Century*: "Babette."

These women incorporate a classically trained sound with a musical theater feel. In other words, they're not singing opera, but they certainly have the chops. With Cook and Andrews, there is an impeccable ability to communicate through incredibly difficult phrases requiring great mastery and control; in a word, perfection. With Ballard and Kahn, there is mastery of comic timing also through difficult phrases done with ease and agility—extraordinary.

Classical Traditional Musical Theater—Male

Bert Convy—*Cabaret*: "Why Should I Wake Up?" John Cullum—*Shenandoah*: "Meditation." Robert Goulet—*Camelot*: "C'est Moi." John Raitt—*The Pajama Game*: "A New Town Is a Blue Town." Also by him— *Carousel*: "Soliloquy."

When it comes to tenors, it doesn't get any better than John Raitt for power and beauty. John Cullum's bass baritone is a force to be reckoned with, and Robert Goulet and Bert Convy represent the quintessential Broadway baritone that has a mixed timbre of classical and belt. Also, check out George Hearn on both the original *Sweeney Todd* cast recording and the original *La Cage Au Folles*.

Classical Contemporary Musical Theater—Female

Kristin Chenoweth—*Let Yourself Go*: "The Girl in 14-G." Also by her—*The Apple Tree*: "Gorgeous." Audra McDonald—*Ragtime*: "Your Daddy's Son." Also by her—

110 in the Shade: "Is It Really Me?" Kelli O'Hara—*The Light in the Piazza*: "The Light in the Piazza."

These women carry on the tradition of classical chops along with a contemporary feel, whether it be Kelli O'Hara's high mixed ping, Audra McDonald's power, or Kristin Chenoweth's chesty twang.

Classical Contemporary Musical Theater-Male

Mandy Patinkin—*Evita*: "Oh What a Circus," "The Money Kept Rolling in (and Out)." Also by him—*Sunday in the Park with George*: "Finishing the Hat." Colm Wilkinson—*Les Misérables*: "Who am I," "Bring Him Home."

These men also carry the classical torch while adhering to the contemporary bent of the music by inducing a twang in their voices that suggests a pop or contemporary feel, not an easy feat. This twang is mostly heard in their upper registers and helps to drive those dramatic points intended in the music to convey greater emotional heights.

Country—New School

Garth Brooks—*No Fences*: "The Thunder Rolls," "Friends in Low Places." Faith Hill—*Breathe*: "Breathe." Shania Twain—*Come On Over*: "You're Still the One."

Although there is an old-school twang present in the sounds of these artists listed here in keeping with the "country" tradition, there is also a contemporary pop and rock influence present that eventually led to a hybrid that you hear more nowadays with artists like Carrie Underwood and Gary LeVox of Rascal Flatts.

Country—Old School

Patsy Cline—*The Patsy Cline Collection*: "Sweet Dreams (of You)," "I Fall to Pieces." Dolly Parton—*Ultimate Dolly Parton*: "I Will Always Love You," "Coat of Many Colors." Hank Williams—*The Ultimate Collection*: "Cold, Cold Heart," "I'm So Lonesome I Could Cry."

This is original country. Although with Patsy Cline what you hear is a more trained, even classical sound than the other two artists, this is country with its original twang and hometown American feel. (Compare both categories of country to hear the subtle differences.)

Crooner—Female

Rosemary Clooney—*Jazz Singer*: "Sophisticated Lady." Also by her—*Rosemary Clooney & Perez Prado: A Touch of Tabasco*: "Mack the Knife." Judy Garland—*Live at Carnegie Hall*: "Alone Together," "San Francisco." K.D. Lang—*Live by Request*: "Black Coffee." Also by her—*Hymns of the 49th Parallel*: "Hallelujah."

Crooners get right to the point. They tell the story through song with great energy, beauty, and musicality. I've included K.D. Lang, one of the few contemporary crooners who had her beginnings in country music. If you check out her canon, you'll see where she married both country with crooning, reminiscent of Patsy Cline. Also check out her album *Ingenue*. As for Garland, there is much to recommend, but I think the Carnegie album encompasses it all: emotion and power running through every lick, every phrase, with a whole lot of humor to boot. With Clooney it's about as straight up as it gets, no bullshit, and beautiful.

Crooner—Male

Tony Bennett—*The Tony Bennett/Bill Evans Album*: "Young and Foolish," "But Beautiful." Bobby Darin—*The Best of Bobby Darin*: "Down With Love," "What a Difference a Day Made." Frank Sinatra—*Only the Lonely*: "One for My Baby." Also by him—*In the Wee Small Hours*: "What is This Thing Called Love?"

The Sinatra selections are of a much younger Sinatra than the ones made for Bennett, however they are both stellar no matter what the age. Bobby Darin, clearly influenced by both of these men, carried on the tradition of crooning, along with others, like Andy Williams. This is a sound that swings and belts but also conveys tender emotion when it has to in a ballad. Like the Ladies of Croon, it's straight up and to the point, while having a helluva lotta fun. Others to listen to are: Nat King Cole, Sammy Davis Jr. and, the fathers of croon, Bing Crosby and Rudy Vallee.

Cry—Pop/Rock/Country

Art Garfunkel—*Bridge Over Troubled Water*: "Bridge Over Troubled Water." Harry Nilsson—*Nilsson Schmilsson*: "Without You." Roy Orbison—*16 Biggest Hits*: "Crying."

Appendix II

These men soar to the top of their ranges with gripping emotion and power. It takes a lot of strength to do this and do it well. They make it sound easy. Garfunkel's the lighter of the three, where Orbison ascends to the heights with sound similar to that of a high mixed belt, making it the anthem for this sound.

Folk

Joan Baez—*Joan Baez*: "House of the Rising Sun." Also by her—*Joan*: "Be Not Too Hard." Don McLean—*Tapestry*: "General Store." Also by him—*Homeless Brother*: "You Have Lived." Peter, Paul & Mary—*The Very Best of Peter, Paul & Mary*: "Early Mornin' Rain," "Blowin' In the Wind." Pete Seeger—*Pete Seeger at the Village Gate*: "Keep Your Hand on the Plow." Also by him—*Pete Seeger's Greatest Hits*: "We Shall Overcome."

This sound comes out of the social conscience of the 1960s. What these people sang about, they were actually living, even if it meant going to jail. They weren't kidding around. Notice how Pete Seeger encourages the audience to sing along with him. It's not about the sound of his voice; it's about the message he's delivering. This sound has a gentle strength to it. It's truthful, courageous, and absolutely humbling. If you're going to mimic it, you better mean what you sing. I also highly recommend: Woody Guthrie—*Dust Bowl Ballads*: "Ain't Got No Home."

Folk Rock—Female

Joni Mitchell—*Court and Spark*: "Down to You." Also by her—*Blue*: "A Case of You." Carly Simon—*Carly Simon*:

"That's the Way I've Always Heard It Should Be." Also by her—*Never Been Gone*: "Let the River Run."

The indie rock chicks of the last two decades have these women to thank for establishing the cool chill sound of folk rock. Here you will hear that yodel sound, where they've allowed their head and chest voices to remain two distinct and separate sounds as opposed to the connection made between both in classical training, what we would call a "mix." Other singers to listen to: Maria Muldaur, Judy Collins, Jewel, and Paula Cole.

Folk Rock—Male

Harry Chapin—*Verities & Balderdash*: "Cat's in the Cradle." Kenny Loggins (of Loggins & Messina) *Sittin In'*: "Danny's Song." James Taylor—*JT*: "Fire and Rain."

Although I've listed Harry Chapin here, he, like Don McLean, had his roots in folk but then crossed over to the pop world of this category. This mellow sound of the 1970s that emanated from the LA scene was a follow-through of the socially conscious songs heard in the 1960s by the likes of Crosby, Stills, Nash, & Young, among others. Others to listen to in this category: The Eagles, Jim Croce, and Gordon Lightfoot, to name a few.

High Mix Belt—Contemporary Musical Theater

Laura Bell Bundy—*Legally Blonde* (Original Broadway Cast Recording): "So Much Better." Eden Espinosa—

Brooklyn (Original Broadway Cast Recording): "Once Upon a Time." Sherie Rene Scott—*Aida* (Original Broadway Cast Recording): "My Strongest Suit."

With the advent of *Evita*, this sound soon found its way onto the Great White Way on a more consistent basis. All three of these women demonstrate it very well, bringing a mix of head resonance with some chest resonance and moving it forward into their masks, making for an exciting sound.

High Mixed Belt—Pop/Rock

Mariah Carey—*Mariah Carey*: "Vision of Love." Celine Dion—*Falling Into You*: "All by Myself." Aretha Franklin—*30 Greatest Hits*: "Chain of Fools," "Respect." Chaka Khan—*I Feel for You*: "Through the Fire." Ann Wilson (of Heart)—*Little Queen*: "Barracuda."

This sound that, I believe, began in the 1960s with such artists as Aretha Franklin and Janis Joplin (although Joplin remains in a category all by herself), picked back up a bit in the 1970s but had a resurgence in the 1980s with females like Deborah Harry and went full throttle into the 1990s. Again, like the ladies of Broadway above, this is the same mixture of head and chest resonance brought high into the mask to make this exciting effect. Others to listen to are: Olivia Newton-John, Patti LaBelle, and Pat Benatar.

Jazz—Scat Singing

Ella Fitzgerald—*The Legendary Decca Recordings*: "Lady Be Good." Johnny Hartman—*John Coltrane and*

Johnny Hartman: "Lush Life." Mel Tormé—*Mel Tormé, Rob McConnell and the Boss Brass*: "Just Friends." Sarah Vaughan—*The Best of "The Divine One" Vaughan*: "Midnight Sun."

These singers can easily be categorized with the other crooners, however, there is a degree of back phrasing (singing a bit behind the tempo), scat singing, and jazz interpretation that makes them distinctly jazz singers.

Roar—Rock/Punk/Metal

Kurt Cobain (of Nirvana)—*Nevermind*: "Smells Like Teen Spirit." James Hetfield (of Metallica)—Master of Puppets: "Master of Puppets." Ozzy Osbourne (of Black Sabbath)—*Paranoid*: "Paranoid." Trent Reznor (of Nine Inch Nails)—*The Downward Spiral*: "March of the Pigs."

Disclaimer: Um, hey, kids, don't try this at home. I call it roar; others might call it...screaming. With the exception of the late, Kurt Cobain, some of these men are still at it, so they obviously know what they're doing, I suggest you do the same.

Rock Tenor—Contemporary Musical Theater

Constantine Maroulis—*Rock of Ages*: "I Wanna Rock." Ted Neeley—*Jesus Christ Superstar*: "Gethsemane." Adam Pascal—*Aida*: "Fortune Favors the Brave."

Here, Ted Neely, who made a career of playing Jesus Christ, leads the pack as a force to be reckoned with. These men, much like the females who work the high mixed belt, learn how to also move this sound high up into their masks while maintaining a tremendous amount of space inside their mouths. It also takes a tremendous amount of strength, as it is supported yelling.

Rock Tenor—Rock/Pop

Freddie Mercury (of Queen)—*Greatest Hits*: "We Will Rock You." Steve Perry (of Journey)—*Greatest Hits*: "Open Arms." Steven Tyler (of Aerosmith)—*Toys in the Attic*: "Walk This Way."

The late, great Freddie Mercury was that of the dramatic and theatrical. He paved the way for many rock tenors included in this category and the men of Broadway mentioned prior. This technique requires a tremendous amount of space in one's mouth, vocal agility, accessibility to the higher resonators (nose, forehead, and crown), and a tremendous amount of strength and stamina in the lower rib cage and abdominal region.

Speak Sing—Country

Johnny Cash—*At Folsom Prison*: "25 Minutes to Go." Willie Nelson—*Stardust*: "Blue Skies."

"Speak sing" says exactly what it means: speaking on pitch. Although with Johnny Cash there is much to listen to, the *At Folsom Prison* album is a must. *Stardust* is an atypical venture for Willie Nelson, but it's a great example of what an artist from another style of music can do to another that is not his or her norm. I think his speak sing style really serves the standards of "The Great American Songbook" well, as he is able to communicate them, making the lyrics the focus.

Speak Sing—Jazz

Chet Baker—*My Funny Valentine*: "Let's Get Lost." Billie Holiday—*The Ultimate Collection*: "Don't Explain." Shirley Horne—*Close Enough for Love*: "I Got Lost in His Arms." Antonio Carlos Jobim—*The Wonderful World of Antonio Carlos Jobim*: "Useless Landscape."

Here again these artists communicate the feelings of whatever they sing so well because it is not about the sound of their voices but what they are communicating. Paradoxically, we love to listen to them sing. Billie Holiday had a way of transcending the listener with her voice right into the very room she was in, singing to her man. Horne, who clearly had more to give vocally, chose to hold back and make the lyric and intent the focus, while Baker and Jobim really knew how to communicate mood with their voices. Another artist to listen to: Michael Franks.

Speak Sing—Musical Theater

Dick Van Dyke—*Mary Poppins*: "Jolly Holiday." Robert Preston—*The Music Man*: "Ya Got Trouble." Also by him—*I Do, I Do*: "Nobody's Perfect" (with Mary Martin).

Elaine Stritch—*Company*: "Here's to the Ladies." Gwen Verdon—*Sweet Charity*: "Charity's Soliloquy."

Here in this style where what you're used to hearing is often a more bright, fuller sound, with lots of vibrato, these musical theater artists take a different route, Robert Preston being the king, in my opinion. Listen for the qualities of personality that emanate: from Gwen Verdon's sweet and quirky, to Elaine Stritchs' brass and sarcasm, and finally to Dick Van Dyke's humor and warmth.

Speak Sing—Pop/Rock

Bob Dylan—*Slow Train Coming*: "Gotta Serve Somebody." Randy Newman—*Twelve Songs*: "Mama Told Me Not to Come."

When listening to these two men, you can easily tell what they sound like when they speak, because their singing voices are so closely aligned to their speaking voices. If you're interested in finding your organic sound, it will behoove you to listen to them as well as all the other artists in this Speak Sing category.

www.ingramcontent.com/pod-product-compliance
Lightning Source LLC
LaVergne TN
LVHW011425080426
835512LV00005B/277